graham greene

The Christian Critic Series

GRAHAM GREENE

Edited by
HARRY J. CARGAS

Contributors

NEVILLE BRAYBROOKE
ROGER C. POOLE
KARL PATTEN
R. W. B. LEWIS
R. E. HUGHES
MARY EVELYN JEFFERSON
CAROLYN D. SCOTT
DOMINICK P. CONSOLO
ALICE MAYHEW

B. HERDER BOOK CO.
314 NORTH JEFFERSON
ST. LOUIS, MISSOURI 63103

The Christian Critic Series is under the general editorship of Harry J. Cargas, Director of the Foreign Student Program, Saint Louis University.

Library of Congress Catalog Card No. 79-79292

With deep love and respect, for

JOACHIM JAMES CARGAS

who searches for truth,

wherever the search may lead.

INTRODUCTION

The essays presented here, some done exclusively for this book, are mature views of a serious author. This, of course, should be understood without comment, yet in the case of Graham Greene, a Christian author who has been maligned and misunderstood by so many Christian critics, this seems to be a necessary clarification.

In preparing this work, I surveyed several books and over two hundred articles on Greene. Most of these, in my judgment, were mediocre at best. So many writings, especially in Catholic periodicals, tended to focus on certain side-issues in Greene's novels. Too often they seemed dedicated to judging the state of the soul of the author who was writing that "junk," "pornography," or "trash." A few would try to make excuses for Greene by pointing out that he really is a surprisingly decent fellow to know. Too many of the former, however, condemned Greene to hell very willingly.

Nor were some critics content with that. Not only was the real person Graham Greene going to hell, but he was to be accompanied by various of his creatures including Pinkie, Scobie, and even the whiskey priest.

So my problem has been to gather certain articles which treated Greene's fiction as fiction. As I have suggested in the opening paragraph, there is a need for the circulation of worthwhile pieces on Greene. It is hoped that this collection contributes to filling that need.

HARRY J. CARGAS

Contents

Carolyn D. Scott

THE URBAN ROMANCE: A STUDY OF GRAHAM GREENE'S THRILLERS

Perhaps one of the most striking revelations Graham Greene makes about himself is the influence of popular literature on his childhood. In several essays: "The Lost Childhood," "The Unknown War," and numerous reviews of individual authors, he drops the names of books that provided him his early inspiration for the literary world and what it could make of life. Since most of the titles he mentions are adventure and mystery stories the influence of this type of fiction on his own work was undoubtedly great. A rather large body of Greene's fiction, the so-called "entertainments," embody the characteristics of this genre. Greene recalls his favorite thrillers, reminiscing among the ornate titles which divined for him the future.

The first volume Greene could read for himself was a mystery about Dixon Brett, detective; and, later, lurking for him upon the family shelves were the adventure stories of Rider Haggard, Captain Brereton, Stanley Weyman, and Marjorie Bowen. The zest of these authors made him want to write and their tone, though obviously modulated, still lives in his fiction. In spite of these observations, however, the most devoted readers of his thrillers have trouble placing them in an established genre. Greene's name is rarely mentioned in conjunction with other great thriller writers: Poe, Doyle, Horung, or Collins. Nor is he cited in general discussions of detective fiction. Seldom are his works placed on the same rack with Ian Fleming's in the local drugstores. Yet, like the escapades of Holmes and .007, the substance of Greene's entertainments readily translates into cinema (all have been made into films) —a fact suggesting that they share with more conventional stories of sleuthing the energy and bluntness of popular art. Yet, like the morally oriented writer that Greene also is, his use of popular art forms constructs for him a statement about what man has made of this chrome-plated, celluloid world. With these ambiguities in mind, we will investigate Greene's tales more closely, hoping to answer the following questions: What is the meaning of the word "entertainment" as Green uses it? What relationship have these entertainments to the mystery story genre? Does this thriller form carry any serious intent?

In discussing the difference between Greene's "entertainments" and "novels," the critics have often seized upon *Brighton Rock* as the line of demarcation splitting his fictional world. This is largely due to a feature of the book's publication history. *Brighton Rock* was first printed by Viking in America as an "entertainment," but was quickly withdrawn, and then reissued without the subtitle. Many have assumed, therefore, that Greene decided the work was more serious than he had earlier regarded it—hence not merely an "entertainment." The internal evidence called to support this view is that the protagonist, Pinkie, is a more fully-developed, Catholicized projection of the socially-twisted Raven, killer-hero of the entertainment, *A Gun For Sale.* And however dubious is the logic of classification here, the contents of *Brighton Rock* have become a scale to weigh the seriousness of Greene's fiction. Mary McCarthy's observations are typical: melodrama and intrigue achieved at the expense of philosophical meditation is interpreted as a lack of seriousness and Greene's fiction is nicely classified accordingly. [1] But scholars might profit from a more careful approach to classification. For if any distinction between the two types of work is valid, I suspect it will have more to do with a shift in the entertainments from theological to political emphasis than with the evaporation of seriousness.

In what is conventionally called the "novels" such as *The Power and the Glory* and *A Burnt-Out Case,* Greene gives us a religious vision with political overtones; whereas his entertainments. *A Gun for Sale* or *Ministry of Fear,* give us a political world with religious implications. The distinction between the two types is less than absolute. In fact, if we give *The Power and the Glory* its American title, *The Labyrinthine Ways,* even this book seems to take on the proportions of the thriller. The New Testament connotations of the British title assures a religious interpretation, while the latter title suggests the melodramatic environment evoked in the Thompson poem. True, the title doesn't change the texture of the work, but flight and betrayal carry profane as well as sacred connotations.

This observation brings up the problem of consistency in the conventional division between novels and entertainments. Do "novels" never entertain? To say that Greene writes novels and entertainments seems much like saying that Wordsworth wrote lyrics and poems. Admittedly we are stuck with Greene's own word "entertainment"—the meaning of which we will study later—but it is well to recall that the subtitle to *Brighton Rock* was simply dropped. It was not changed from "entertainment" to "novel." Greene may have thought his thrillers a special kind of performance, but significantly the rest of his fiction is given no tag at all. This, as well as several other considerations, should dissuade us from making too much of the distinction.

In spite of these difficulties, several critics have attempted to classify the elements that seem to distinguish the entertainments from the novels. Francis Kunkel, in his chapter on the entertainments, observes that they are "psychological thrillers" with highly melodramatic plots focusing on a few characters and featuring subtle perception, ingenius situation, a lasting sense of suspense, swift narrative, and masterful style. Furthermore, says Kunkel: "None of the thrillers disturbs the reader's complacency nor drugs him with powerful, longlasting aftereffects, as the novels do."[2] Somehow I get the nagging feeling that the reader whose complacency is not disturbed by the plaster and tinsel world that spawns a Raven only to squash him like an ugly bug in a gas mask who disturbs the Christmas spirit, or by a Harry Lime bleeding against the sewer grating whimpering like a dying rabbit, remains insensitive to much of our social disorientation that so disturbs Greene. But later Kunkel points out that Greene's modern thrillers expose profound moral problems and links them with the crime and punishment tradition of Dostoyevsky and Conrad. A. A. de Vitis adds to the list of definitions the lack of serious religion in the entertainments.[3] The thrillers, he says, are secularized presentations of the problem of good and evil. He hedges around this point, however, perhaps to avoid it after all, and claims for the entertainments everything from abandoning religion for superstition to maintaining a "religious sense" instead of a "religious point of view." David Pryce-Jones confuses our conceptions of the entertainment with the note that the heroes of the entertainments "make their disavowal of religious interest quite explicit," thus stripping them of religious purpose.[4] The total picture of an entertainment, then, implies a melodrama masterfully, suspensefully, ingeniously written, lacking proper religious tone and seriousness, yet focusing on moral problems as the core.

Mulling over this definition, I find little there that could not be said of any number of novels and novelists. Masterful style, suspense, melodrama, and moral problems belong not only to the total body of Greene's fiction but to just about anybody's. Although the critics protest that the difference between melodrama in the entertainments and religion in the novels is merely a matter of degree, one cannot say that the elements of fiction are to be weighed and measured like a sack of grain. De Vitis cites the passage in *A Gun for Sale* where Anne answers Raven's question about belief in God with, "It's like crossing your fingers when you walk under a ladder," to illustrate his point that religion is exchanged for superstition in the thrillers. But Sarah in *The End of the Affair* believes blindly; she would accept Christ even if he were a mere conjuring of Pilate. In Greene's fiction it doesn't seem to matter if you cross your fingers or your whole body, so long as you raise the question of God. I suspect that the real problem here is that the critics do not know what to do with a man who seems to write frivolities in deference to his more serious work. The first problem we must resolve, then, is one of tone, texture, and form. How seriously did Greene take the thriller form himself?

There is an amusing scene from *The Third Man* which seems to represent this matter allegorically through the implications it carries of an author's relationship to his critics and to the realities of experience with which both author and critic are concerned. Rollo Martins, alias Buck Dexter, writer of cheap westerns, is mistaken for Benjamin Dexter, writer of religious novels, and trapped into delivering a little lecture to a Vienna literary society. Because his audience lacks knowledge of English and American culture, he is able to get away with the deception—not that he really wants to be recognized as Benjamin Dexter but that this provides a convenient way to stay shy of the police for a while. So he is carried through a hilarious, half-drunken discussion of his career, the society asking questions to Benjamin Dexter, author of the *Curved Prow,* and he replying as Buck Dexter, author of *The Lone Rider of Santa Fe.* Here we might see Greene's double self arguing with the critics who view him as one personality yet get answers from another. Martins seriously cites Zane Grey as his mentor only to find the literary society thinks he is joking. Mr. Crabbins, the chairman, smooths things over by saying he must have meant the poet, Thomas Gray, "a gentle, mild, subtle genius—one can see the affinity." He then goes on to explain that Zane Grey is a writer of cheap westerns.

"He was just a popular entertainer."
"Why the hell not?" Martins said fiercely.
"Oh, well, I merely meant—"
"What was Shakespeare?"
Somebody with great daring said, "A poet."
"Have you ever read Zane Grey?"
"No I can't say—"
"Then you don't know what you are talking about."

Though the talk then turns to Joyce, Martins has made his impression and someone whispers to Crabbin, "How do you spell Zane?" Having perceived the shallow literary knowledge of the group, Martins feels confident in autographing Benjamin Dexter's *Curved Prow* with, "From B. Dexter, author of *The Lone Rider of Santa Fe.*" Though his gesture befuddles the group, it is not exactly a lie. In like manner the considerations often meant for Graham Greene, author of *The Heart of the Matter,* are directed at Greene, author of *Stamboul Train.*

During the forum, someone asks Martins the title of his current novel. He replies, "The Third Man," while inwardly contemplating the real thriller he is living concerning the strange facts surrounding Lime's supposed death. The admirers of Benjamin Dexter, religious author, might imagine that the title refers to a Biblical source, the road to Emmaeus, rather than one of the facts in the mystery Martins is investigating. Greene himself must have anticipated the confusion of the symbol mongers who seized upon the title of the actual novel and thus viewed Harry Lime as a Christ figure, since they are both "the third man." But the title could also refer to a more secular and modern source, Eliot's *Waste Land,* which depicts the fog and decay that turn up again in Greene's novel. Vienna, like the Unreal City, contains "the third who walks always beside you," in the half-diabolical figure of Lime who tempts Martins to deal in the black market. So we see that there is a good deal of confusion over the amount of serious projection of life the thriller form can bring. According to some critics it must be made into religious images in order to be successful.

Martin's authorship of entertaining fiction leads to little pleasantries about his work by his acquaintances. Calloway praises Martins as a writer of fiction for his way with Westerns—a "trick of tension," he calls it. It is this knack that allows him to hunt out with sensitivity the irregularities surrounding the accidental death in a politically confused Vienna. Sleuthing has become the way of modern life. The irony that he is composing fiction from what he knows to be the real world—a subject we suspect Benjamin Dexter's *Curved Prow* is not about—leads us to a very important consideration about Greene's attitudes toward thriller fiction.

The thriller form is the shape of the modern predicament, not only in its portrayal of flight and pursuit, but in its treatment of the search for identity among the real and the fantastic. Wormold, the little vacuum cleaner salesman in *Our Man in Havana,* has spent a lot of energy fabricating a plausible spy report out of maps, *Time,* and drawings of his vacuum cleaners just for money and a little joke on the Secret Service. He is horrified when the fictional characters of his subagents become enfleshed only to be murdered. They were formerly only names from the phone book. Suddenly, in a Pirandello-like situation, he must warn them of their involvment lest the fiction get the upper hand and annihilate them all. He then comes to realize how real the thriller world can be. His secretary, Beatrice, reminds him:

"We're back in the *Boy's Own Paper* world, that's all. You can count yourself lucky. . . . It might have been the *Sunday Mirror.* . . . The world is modelled after the popular magazines nowadays. . . . The question we have to consider is to which paper *they* belong."

The little melodrama of Raul, the drunken pilot, had more bearing on his real life than Wormold suspects until it is too late and the real Raul is killed.

Greene's personal feelings on the matter take somewhat of the same ironical tone. His fiction is very closely parallel to popular fiction. He had already noted the impact of comic book characters in the *Rover, Hotspur, Skipper,* and *Girl's Own Paper.* There is an eternal desire for adventure stories—"the war that will never come to an end,"—the fiendish devices of Vultz, mad German inventor, the heroics of Nick Ward against Nazi leader Dr. Poyner. This world of mad engineers, twisted Nazis, fantastic heroes from the rank and file of British subjects is also the world of Greene.

Greene's use of popular forms of crime come from both slick fiction and films. His characters are drawn with the bold strokes of a comic book: Raven with his hare lip and tattered coat, the manageress of *Confidential Agent* with spots around her mouth and gold teeth, Myatt with his box of currants and oiled hair—blue-black like a Clark Kent who never turns Superman. Melodrama surrounds them like murky clouds: the conventional deflowering of the chorus girl, Coral, in the train compartment; sentimental songs—"It's only Kew to you/But it's paradise to me," "Your photograph/Is just the sweetest half;" the appearance of a happy ending, Rose sailing off with D ("You'll be dead very soon, you needn't tell me that, but *now* . . ."), Anne turning to Mather after gazing over London's cheap Christmas shops ("Oh," she said, with a sigh of unshadowed happiness, "we're home.") Much of the environment the characters find themselves in is straight out of ads in cheap magazines: Mr. Cholmondeley's monstrous Christmas tree; the chorus panto, "Christmas for Two;" Myatt's currants; the Atomic Pile vacuum cleaner.

Greene also borrows popular cinema technique. He spent a good part of the 30's reviewing films where detective and spy stories abounded. In an early review of a film study he noted the importance of montage as a modern medium of art. Its effect on literature, close to melodrama, Greene observed in such works as the *Waste Land,* a poem whose mood is not far from his own fiction. [5] *Stamboul Train* develops an interesting montage effect as

Greene cuts from one contrasting conversation to another on the dining car—from cries of the waiters, to Hungarian cricket, to beer, to currants and love. Like a Hitchcock movie the compartments sometimes assume a supernatural quality with their contrasting lights as they flash by in the night.

> Human beings floated like fish in golden water, free from the urge of gravity, flying without wings, transparent, in a glass aquarium. Ugly faces and misshapen bodies were transmuted, if not into beauty, at least into grotesque forms fashioned by a mocking affection.

In Greene's fiction there are also grotesque devices belonging to the cinema: Mather on the platform lowered from a roof to shoot Raven; a murder in Mrs. Bellair's seance; rapid cuts to a mocking background of profane music—"What did Aladin say"—that follows Mr. Cholmondeley; reflected scenes, D discovered in a mirror by the manageress. All of the entertainments have been made into movies. Greene himself wrote some of the scripts: *Loser Takes All* and *Our Man in Havana. The Third Man,* made in reverse from script to novel, is surprisingly less cinematic except for the sewer chase where gun shots echo and torches flash.

Most critics fail to appreciate the art of these scenes. John Atkins, for instance, calls this random technique "the curse of the film," because it is dependent on some trick or gagline. He wonders at the praise of the "filmic quality" to be found in Greene's "worst work" and asserts that in Greene's later work excellence is achieved by adherence to the rules of the art of fiction. [6]

But this machinery of fiction writing enables Greene to dramatize a very real world. The kaleidoscopic effect of sordid images from popular fiction gives a modern tone to the novels. The popular form does not preclude the possibility of seriousness; rather, it puts us in touch with life. Arthur Rowe's dream tells him thrillers are like real life. Gone are the days of novels about tea on the lawn. Benjamin Dexter may be grounded in neutral Stockholm, but Buck Dexter discovers the grit of real experience in war-torn Vienna. The world of the popular magazine is closer to real life than the poet's; Zane Grey, not Thomas Gray, leads Rollo to Harry Lime. The popular novelist, Savory, observes in an interview on the Stamboul Train: "A poet's an individualist. He can dress as he likes; he depends only on himself. A novelist depends on other men; he's an average man with the power of expression. 'E's a spy."

How ironically close this cheap, popular world is to stark reality of war comes home to agent D in *Confidential Agent.*

He stared gloomily away across the little hotel hall: an aspidistra on stilts, an umbrella rack in the form of a shell case. He thought: We could make an industry out of that, with all the shells we have at home. Empty shell cases for export. Give a tasteful umbrella stand this Christmas from one of the devastated cities.

Like Wormold's fiction, the imitation becomes hideously like the real in its cheap appeal. A political seriousness creeps in. The war against authority, the caricatured villians like Dr. Forester and his insane asylum, Cholmondeley and his toffees, Captain Segura and his cigarette case made of human skin, all are part of that vast conspiracy—the "ministry of fear" that looms larger than a single novel—like S.P.E.C.T.R.E., grotesque, absurd, yet startlingly enfleshed with the sadism of the fascist mentality. Greene, like Beatrice, knows that *they* really do come from *Boy's Own Paper* and it is this game that we must reckon with. Greene adapts his ideas to the thriller form because it is *ex populo,* and because it deals with human justice truthfully. It is not a bad thing to be driven back to the blood in such thriller movies like *I Am A Fugitive From A Chain Gang*. In the 1930's, when Greene began his writing career, the people doted on thriller movies in Germany, England, and America. They knew that conspiracy was afoot and they weren't going to miss a spine-tingling moment of it. Greene knew it too, but he also observed that English thrillers were:

> doomed from the start by middle-class virtue, by gentleman cracksmen and stolen plans and Mr. Wu's. We have to go further back than this, dive below the polite level, to something nearer the common life. And isn't it better to have as your subject "life nasty, brutish, and short" than the more pompous themes the censor denies us? [7]

Mere mechanics of solving the puzzle is not enough. Detectives like Mather never learn about men like Raven; it's only a job. But we learn because Greene carries us into the world of cheap injustice to Raven in the chrome office or Christ in the plaster manger.

Although many critics have noticed that Greene claims importance to the influence of such childhood adventure stories as *King Solomon's Mines* and *Viper of Milan,* they do not make much of these adventures that "colour and explain the terrible living world." [8] What was this "enormous brutality and dispairing romanticism" that so attracted him to writing? As we have accepted amorous Jack Donne and solemn John Donne as the same personage, perhaps we can also accept Greene the entertainer and Greene the meditator in one. Even though Greene employs the metaphor of paradox to convey the ambiguities of character in the modern world, we still have the ever lurking problem concerning his decision to use the word "entertainment" in a specialized manner.

The word as Greene applies it to fiction cannot be found in a similar definition in the OED. The two definitions that are closest to his supposed intentions are: "The action of occupying a person's attention agreeably," and, "A public performance or exhibition intended to interest or amuse." Nowhere is a type of fiction named under "entertainment." Fiction is surely meant to be agreeable even in a negative sense, so the word does not separate the thriller from the novel form. Greene uses the word elsewhere, specifically in the "Introduction" to *The Third Man,* which would tend to connect it with the second definition cited. "I held the view that an entertainment of this kind was too light an affair to carry the weight of an unhappy ending." But of course he was referring to the movie here, and not the novel. The context of that passage, arising out of his disagreement with director Reed, concerns the indeterminacy of the movie's end and the cynical overtones it might convey to the audience. They were resolved with the unity of zither music, a not altogether happy instrument; but the novel itself does not contain music, nor even the subtitle "entertainment," though it is almost universally regarded as one.

Are we then to assume that Greene has played a little joke on us? Did he make a division in his fiction that doesn't exist for the mere fun of it? Or did he write for money as he claimed for *Stamboul Train?* If that is so then Greene must have found himself much in the same position as Wormold who feared his characters had become so real that they would come out of the very walls at his bidding. His precedent for using the word that implies interest in mere amusement can be compared to a similar use by another author, Henry James, one Greene admired very much and one whose serious intent in the writing of fiction cannot be disputed.

In his discussion of James's thriller, *The Turn of the Screw,* Greene claims that the author's description of his novella as "a fairy-tale pure and simple," something seasonable for Christmas, is a "disingenuous description" of the overtones of spiritual evil he discovers there. [9] Greene seems to think that the materialist in James has caused him to recoil from the spiritual and made him to be less than frank with the significance of the spirit of evil that has crept into his novels. James goes on to describe his own novel as an "*amusette* to catch those not easily caught . . . the jaded, the disillusioned, the fastidious." An *amusette* is a child's toy, a diversion and, like the word "entertainment," in no sense means a fictional genre. *Amu-*

sette rather implies a frivolous tone, one also found in Greene's word. Like Greene, James has employed a device to ironically minimize the worth of his production. The "catch" is a moral one despite its seemingly frivolous appearance. James's identification with the "cold artistic calculation" of diversionary literature — detective stories and the like—still recognizes the worth of roaming over "an annexed but independent world in which nothing is right save as we rightly imagine it." James wrote many other gothic romances in the thriller frame of the novel, where imagination and reality linger together on a murky border where men are taken for ghosts. Taking after James's romance pattern, Greene's entertainments hang about that same ambiguous world of good and evil, the pursuer and the pursued. But in Greene's novels, behind the Hound of the Baskervilles lurks the Hound of Heaven, and it is no accident that a mystic counter-part follows the fiery-eyed gothic monster of the moors. As the religious aspect of Henry James lies in his sense of evil, so likewise in Greene's thrillers. The genre of mystery stories take as their focal point the chase and flight through the labyrinth of the city, an obsession of modern fiction. The heroes of *Crime and Punishment, The Secret Agent,* and *The Trial* find themselves chasing and being chased through images of stone and steel.

The mystery story as the expression of the "poetry of modern life" is explored by another Catholic writer of thrillers, G. K. Chesterton. He notes astutely that:

> A city is . . . more poetic even than a countryside, for while Nature is a chaos of unconscious forces, a city is a chaos of conscious ones. . . . But there is no stone in the street and no brick in the wall that is not actually a deliberate symbol—a message from some man. . . . [10]

Although Chesterton's own mysteries do not follow this pattern—Father Brown is hardly the hero who "crosses London with something of the loneliness and liberty of a prince in a tale of elfland"—he observes the truth about the focus and celebration of the modern mystery story. It is a truth that Greene most assuredly shares. The seedy side of life is a point of view that the modern author is compelled to take. On his voyage from civilization to the primitive to recall "at which point we went astray," Greene reflects:

> Today our world seems peculiarly susceptible to brutality. There is a touch of nostalgia in the pleasure we take in gangster novels, in characters who have agreeably simplified their emotions that they have begun living again at a level below the cerebral. We, like Wordsworth, are living after a war and a revolution, and these half-castes fighting with bombs between the cliffs of skyscrapers seem more likely than we to be aware of Proteus rising from the sea. [11]

The romance of the city takes on a peculiar caste with Greene. It is not the elfland, Dickensian London of carolers and mail coaches that is associated with the Holmes fiction. Greene has always been appalled by what he calls the "seediness" in the glitter of chrome. The city, product of an insipid middle class, is the home of intrigue and bedeviled protagonists of the entertainments. The intrigue involves the individual's revolt against mass culture, what we've made of the primitive. Although these individuals are alone in a hostile city, it bares friendly memories—sometimes ironic memories. Confidential agent D, fresh from the terror of a civil war on the continent, wanders over London looking at shops and contemplating the contrast in this complacent country and his own blood-torn one, not without affection.

> He walked, enjoying the sense of unreality—the shop windows full of goods, no ruined houses anywhere, women going into Buzzards for coffee. . . . A pale winter sun shone, and the scarlet buses stood motionless all down Oxford Street: there was a traffic block. What a mark, he thought, for enemy planes! It was always about this time that they came over. But the sky was empty—or nearly empty. One winking, glittering little plane turned and dived on the pale clear sky, drawing in little puffy clouds a slogan: "Keep Warm with Ovo."

No war slogan could be so prophetic to an England unaware. Greene's negative romance of the city, the alien wanderer adventuring through the conscious stone puzzle man has made of his civilization, adopts the second phrase of, "God made the country, man made the town." He embraces the fantastic world of cheap restaurants and hotels to discover its source, the men who made and share its litter-strewn streets. Even Raven who finds London distasteful looks wistfully from the train as the city recedes into the background: the signal box, the cocoa on the stove, the long line of blackened houses against the sky. Greene can admire the appalling, the repulsive, the tawdry as part of the "chaos of conscious forces" be it war-scarred London, the sewers of Vienna, or the back streets of Havana. And this chaos Greene welds together into a shapeless city with a dream-like atmosphere coming from his intense childhood.

Greene's fascination with what man has made of the primitive, a "supernatural cruelty" we have exchanged for a gangster brutality of civilization is in keeping with an underlying impetus in the craft of mystery stories. Greene is close to the sources of buried aggression impulses, often noted as the reason for reading mysteries, since his own childhood was filled with memories of violence, suicides on the street, dreams of horror, a dead dog in the bottom of his pram. But he would take the claims of the detective as a moralist who relieves these impulses not too seriously. He turns to the revolver in the corner cupboard, symbol of his own personal bout with violence, with mixed feelings of awe and cynicism. The moral of this essay on his attempt to experience sensation establishes much of the rebel nihilist that is in Greene. His adolescent flirtation with Russian roulette formulates itself against the sterility of boredom after indulging in sessions of psychoanalysis. The act of rebellion restored his aesthetic interest in the visual, not of flowers and sunsets, but in the litter-strewn wilderness of the Common, "gorse, old trenches, abandoned butts"—"the unchanging backcloth of most adventures of childhood."[12] And it is Greene's experiences with childhood adventure stories that has provided the atmosphere: the search for the death-like image of Gagool the *King Solomon's Mines,* "her bare yellow skull, the wrinkled scalp that moved and contracted like the hood of a cobra"[13] among the repulsive paths of the world. Like James, he fears the novel whose social context has been "washed clean by the laboratory taps," that knows little of the ghostly terror, "the something that has got to come in."

The primitive, romantic image pervades the early and recurring dreams and later his novels as a "force exerted on a door, an influence that drifted after me upstairs and pressed against the windows,"—an old Arab, a half-caste, a Chinese detective. There is a paradox in the dream atmosphere—a "cruel and reassuring presence" Greene calls it, a power we knew in childhood and could not escape. It was only in the jaded years of adulthood that the sick, scientific dream, washed clean of the primitive adventure, crept in. "Evil" came to his dreams: "the man with the gold teeth and rubber surgical gloves; the old woman with ringworm; the man with his throat cut dragging himself across the carpet to the bed." They are the images of decay, neurosis, and diabolical authority. In Africa Greene gets near to the earlier terror in the form of a shaman, the bush devil, who in the primitive represents a power of both good and evil, but in his return to civilization Greene notices that the science of the rational, the unsuperstitious has washed the culture clean of the "finer terror on which we might have built."[14]

Greene's disposition to depict the atmosphere of dream and mystery, the romance of the primitive terror, also links his entertainments to the gothic mystery of the late nineteenth century. The heroes of the latter wander the city to solve the riddle of the ghostly terror of their dreams. They are both the pursuer and the pursued. Unlike the detectives of a later generation who coldly rationalize the puzzle with mental gymnastics, the heroes of gothic fiction seek themselves in their tale of terror. But most modern detective stories pride themselves in being the "one form of novel today which does not insist that we must lose ourselves to find ourselves; the one form of contemporary literature in which our cold impersonality need never fail."[15]

This insistence upon scientific detachment—an undeniably attractive escape mechanism which makes the typical detective story something like a crossword puzzle or a game of chess—is not escape for Greene because it represents the culture washed clean. He returns to the old metaphoric terror, for the supernatural allegory he finds in concrete things. In his hands the detective's detailed game of chess turns into a morality play with the pieces taking on significance as they move. The entertainment is not in the puzzle but in the players. The melodrama in the entertainment, cheap as its emotional play might be, consciously works against the legalistic mood of the modern detective novels of Queen, Gardiner, and Christie. There is a return to the old romance of the convict hero like Jean Valjean and the picaresque highwayman like Robin Hood and Jonathan Wild. Arthur Rowe is as guilty of a modern social problem, pity, as the Frenchman is of hunger; and Harry Lime is like the comic Vice of the medieval stage—"Marlowe's devils wore squibs attached to their tails: evil was like Peter Pan. . . ."

Greene's novels are not patterned after the Newgate Calendar as were earlier detective stories: his characters are not to be found in police files nor does the solution depend on the scientific method of Scotland Yard. His heroes are jaded and disillusioned. They flee from the middle-class delight in crime detection that keeps one's possessions safe. The desire for a power structured authority to intervene is the dream they struggle against: the man with the surgical gloves—the evil in prim, formulaic convention—presses against the door. Raven's crime is misunderstood by the fearful populace of the small town he terrorizes. He is hunted down by a bumbling police detective whose conventional assumptions distorts the motives of all concerned, including those of his own fianceé. She, too, is under suspicion because her association with the criminal can't be explained by the police handbook. Fleeing the police, agent D learns first hand of middle class fatuity as he finds his way into the apartment of an Oxford Grouper, for whom, "God is in the candlelight/ Watching in your home."

The flight from the middle class power structure is a flight from conditional responses and mechanical attitudes, the threat of inflexible conventions, in Greene's words, "what man has made of the primitive." D, even in his posture as a scholar, embodies this struggle to recover the true primitive and with it a more meaningful grasp of evil. As his very specialized gloss of the *Song of Roland* suggests, this renewed understanding of evil promises to furnish a new ethic. His reading of *Roland*, of course, depends on the obscure version of the poem which he has spent his academic career researching. In this version, Oliver emerges as the real hero and Roland descends. Roland is guilty of sacrificing his men to preserve his personal and conventional rules of glory. He waits until all his men are killed before he sounds his horn to recall Charlemagne. In the standard versions, Oliver strikes down Roland by accident; but in the Berne MS Oliver kills him with full knowledge in his anger over his friend's display. Thus Oliver dies hating a man he loves—an inconclusive end to a once heroic epic.

According to D's reading, Oliver becomes the prototype of the modern anti-hero. Witness his comments to Rose: "But you can see how that version didn't appeal—in the castles—at the banquets, among the dogs and mead and beakers: the jongleurs had to adapt it to meet the tastes of the medieval nobles, who were quite capable of being Rolands in a small way." Rose, whose father owns the coal company D is trying to persuade to aid his cause, remarks, "My father, of course, would be like one of your barons—all for Roland." And indeed he ends up supporting the middle-class fascist side of agent L. Even the miners to whom D preaches about the international brotherhood of the socialist cause turn out to be Rolands, inasmuch as their personal greed makes them callously complacent towards their suffering comrades abroad. Only the hoodlum gangsters are interested in sabotaging the mine, all for the wrong reasons. Like Oliver, D has no choice but to lash out against those who ought to be his friends. When the plan fails, he is left to the vengeance of a righteous crowd fresh from the evening church meeting where they have prayed meaninglessly for the homeless and destitute. They find satisfaction in detecting and delivering into the hands of the London police the criminal and disturbing elements. The hunter's delight crystalizes in the cold detachment of the puzzle and clue, the hunted in preserving the self—D in the shed, Czinner in the abandoned warehouse, Raven in the garage, Rowe in the shelter: "The foxes have their holes, but the son of man . . ." ring out the bells to Raven.

Greene's hunted heroes, like those of romantic mystery fiction as a whole, struggle between two kinds of evil—the primitive evil, James's "fairy-tale side of life" or Maritan's "creative unconscious"—and the jaded evil of a representative superego that gradually paralyzes us as we grow into civilization. To see the significance of this view, we must take it as a reacting against the kind of horror story that provides cheap thrills while it moves towards a pat solution, often full of authoritarian implications. As we have noted earlier, twentieth-century European society doted on detective films. Siegfried Kracauer relates the German interest in them to the people's desire for the authority figure, the scientific, the puzzle solving, the simple ending—"made to suit" like the Roland story. Behind them lears the face of Dr. Caligari, the evil man of science like Greene's man in the surgical gloves and gold teeth. Caligari mesmerized the whole country with his trick, changing the sheer horror of the mad scientist into the benevolent tyranny of a psychiatrist. In the film, *The Cabinet of Dr. Calig-*

ari, a young man, Francis, who is convinced Caligari is using a somnambulist in an evil experiment to murder innocent victims discovers that it is all his insane fantasy about the psychiatrist who is treating him in the asylum. The audience is led to accept docilely this facile explanation: the man who questions the intentions of authority must surely be mad. His fantasy has attacked the secure position of the bourgeois because it finds the source of evil to be interior—credulity in the slight of hand—and not in external causes. It is significant, I think, that the inspiration for the original script, which vindicates the young man's accusation about Caligari, was the murder of a young girl by a "respectable bourgeois."

The figure of the evil doctor takes shape from an earlier fairy-tale, Hoffmann's *Der Sandman.* Greene is undoubtedly familiar with the common archetypes these two alchemists come from. The cruel and reassuring presence of the Sandman, who scratches out children's eyes and carries them off to the moon turns to evil in the form of Dr. Coppelius when Nathaniel discovers his rites of alchemy with his father. Greene's own experience with the Sandman occured in the bush country of Africa. He comes near to the witch of his dreams embodied in the shaman bush devil. ". . . My servants sat in their shuttered hut with their hands over their eyes and someone beat a drum and a whole town stayed behind closed doors while the big bush devil—whom it would mean blindness to see—moved between the huts." [16] When Greene returns to civilization the bush devil has been transformed by a transfixed bourgeoise into the figurehead of the Third Reich.

How close, then, fairy-tale is to reality is the burden of Greene's entertainments. The relation of Greene's entertainments to the two types, the fairy-tale and popular mystery fiction, includes more than just form. Both the fantasies of the romantic heroes, Nathanial and Francis, contain the germ of social protest against authority figures. But their dependence on imagination, their refusal to conform, their search for identity amid confusion, are not merely part of the romance. These characteristics are part of the psychology of resistance to authority seen in the figures of Caligari and Coppelius. Their witch-like presence can be found in the evil that haunts Greene's dreams. The early shamans of primitive culture were the first authority figures and the modern demogogue still practices the magic rituals of religious medicine with his promises to cure the ills of society. The difference is in their cold detachment. Personal dignity and self-quest are denied as the proper goals of men. The desire for a unified, ordered, moral world surpasses all other considerations of what man has made of man. The refusal to examine the man within originates in complete denial of romantic values as well as democratic ones. The visionary gleam and the ability of every man to find his own destination have no place in the authoritarian society. I have already pointed out Greene's association with the romantic, populist movement in his specialized use of the thriller form. His attempts to return to that old terror necessarily leads his novels into the realm of the social: a reassessment of the nature of the early nursery witch of his inner self contrasts it with the other, later sources of external evil, the evils of the social order.

The politics of Greene's thrillers, then, consists of the impulsive rejection of smug pseudo-rational authority figures. Nightmare ghouls, like the Nazi Dr. Forester of *Minister of Fear* officiating over the minds of his patients, like Caligari, float through Greene's entertainments pressing their evil pleasantries upon the unsuspecting. In *A Gun for Sale* Mr. Cholmondeley sucks on toffee with his gold-filled teeth and dreams up political murders that will get his company rich. As he attempts to murder Anne who asks too many questions, "she fought against his hands, strong, and soft and sticky with icing sugar." In *Confidential Agent,* Mr. K and the manageress press D for the papers authorizing his mission. "The manageress's black skirt was close to his mouth, dusty like cat's fur. He wanted to scream, but the weight of human dignity lay like a gag over his tongue. . . . Her breath was all cheap scent and nicotine—half female and half male." The smell of "flowers gone bad" comes from Greene's dream of evil. Harry Lime too is like an old miasmic devil disappearing and appearing in the Vienna fog. He takes Rollo up on a huge abandoned ferris wheel while offering him the world of the black market, then disappears down a kiosk to the sewers below. Greene's fantasies have brought these characters into being. The shadow of evil come from within.

The reality of the nightmare world come to Arthur Rowe between waking and sleeping in the bomb shelter. He dreams that he is trying to convince his mother that he killed his wife. "Life isn't real any more. Tea on the lawn, evensong, croquet. . . . People write about it as if it still went on; lady novelists describe over and over again in books of the month, but it's not there any more." In this tea time moment of stability and security of the dream Arthur tries to convince her of the reality of the nightmare world of the blitz. "It sounds like a thriller, doesn't it?—but the thrillers are like life—more like life than you are, this lawn, your sandwiches, that pine. You used to laugh at the books Miss Savage read—about spies, and murders and violence, and wild motor car chases, but dear, that's real life: Its what we've all made of the world since you died." Greene has never left the discovery of "a dim conception of the appalling mysteries of life moving through a ravaged world" that first crossed the border of the green baize door of his father's study in his childhood.

The role of fantasy in Greene's thrillers does not exclude the social context. It is true that Greene drops a puzzling array of religious articles throughout the pages: Jansenist crucifixes, plaster manger scenes, votive candles. This seeming religious atmosphere along with the interiorization of sin has lead some critics to view Greene's Catholicism as more central than any other consideration. One has said about the entertainments: "He will not pause to consider that sin is, in a very true sense, social evil, civil disruption, familial dissolution." Greene rather thinks, says the critic, that sin is "evil and rotteness and stench." He is concerned with "Heaven and Hell" more than "good and evil." [17] Viewing the novels with the information considered earlier in this paper about Greene's notion of evil, these words make little sense. A better explanation comes from an article which links Greene with an author of thrillers. Robert Louis Stevenson. Charles Brady sees two sorts of allegories in the thriller melodrama type: "a local allegory of our times, where rival political theories play hare and hounds across the page; the other a more universal allegory, with the Hound of Heaven in pursuit, and the quarry the soul of man." [18] The thriller form with its visionary quality still cannot avoid the social, political commentary upon the source of man's crimes. None of Greene's entertainments ignore the political upheaval of Europe through the thirties and forties. Dr. Czinner of *Stamboul Train* is wanted by fascist forces in Budapest for perpetrating a socialist uprising; Myatt of the same novel discovers anti-Semiticism in Eastern Europe; agent D works against fascist elements in a continental civil war similar to Spain's; Raven is hired by two greedy factory owners to kill the socialist minister of another country so that they can profit by a war; Rowe struggles against the Nazi Ministry of Fear; Martins discovers Lime participating in selling watered penicilin in post-war Vienna; and Wormold fabricates a "they" more fantastic than the ever-suspicious Secret Service could conjure. The central figures in these entertainments (*Loser Takes All* is excepted because it is merely a pleasantry) encounter political authority in one form or another and must make an ethical decision about it. Even Raven, whose criminality is more clear cut than the others, commits his second murder to rectify, in his own code, the injustice of the first. When he discovers that the minister he has assassinated was a friend of the people and could have done good in the world he sees as so corrupt, Raven takes up his vengeance with the renewed vigor of a man crazed with social injustice. The appeal of this violent approach to political justice might be seen in a description of the appeal of Bogart, whose performances often paralleled Raven's actions, as the "Insider gone sour," "a romantic hero inconceivable in any time but ours." Through this favorite screen hero of the thriller movies we can see Greene dipping into the seedy, the popular mediums to find a suitable frame of reference for the social situation of the thirties. "He (Bogart) is the first romantic hero who used the gangster's means to achieve our ends. And this character was suddenly very precious in the age of violence, for it satisfied a quiet, desperate need of the engulfed, ordinary citizen." [19] Raven's social disorientation comes from a hare lip which his family could not afford to fix well, and the orphan's home where no one was beaten on Christmas day and he learned about Christ. He sees Christ as a victim of the same social outrages.

> They made him a god because they could feel fine about it all: They didn't have to consider themselves responsible for the raw deal they'd given him. . . . He stood there . . . at the swaddled child with a horrified tenderness—"the little bastard"—because he was educated and knew what the child was in for: . . . with no one even to draw a knife on his side when the soldiers came for him in the garden.

Such physical loyalty is little accorded Christ by his followers with their filled Christmas shops, their easy moral judgment, their fear of the unknown.

Although Raven fails to understand Christ in any religious sense—he mocks the word Christian—he is aware of more of the social ills than those who would blindly eradicate him from the social scene as a mere killer. Raven knows that modern society has "twisted his words" to make them what they will. No one turns the other cheek these days.

Another religious character, Dr. Czinner of *Stamboul Train,* finds himself in strange alliance with Christ in his political struggles with the Nazis, whose power Europe is just barely beginning to comprehend. He mistakes a thief for a police spy in his train compartment. With his eye on a silver cross on the man's watch chain swinging back and forth with the man's movement, he has a momentary vision of the social implications of the way of the cross.

> . . . it might have been lurching to the human stride, and for a moment Dr. Czinner flattened himself against the wall of a steep street to let the armoured men, the spears, and the horses pass, and the tired tortured man. He had not died to make the poor contented, to bind the chains tighter; his words had been twisted.

Czinner's vision figures in his decision to return to Budapest at the risk of his own life. It seems relevant to note here that Greene makes us aware that although Christ was tried upon ethical grounds, his death was a political one executed by the largest power structure of the time. His crucifixion not only renders unto God but also unto Caesar. He has been made the scapegoat for all ills, interior and exterior.

Although Greene conceives of his characters as either tough guys whose violence matches a violent age, or as agents whose political mission can be envisioned in religious exercise, there is yet another way to view the victim of authority. When Wormold observes how his fabricated position as a spy has implicated his friend, Dr. Hasselbacher, so deeply that the police search his apartment, he observes: "There was always another side to a joke, the side of the victim." Earlier it is his sense of humor that allows him to foil the police authorities whose suspicions lie in their own nightmares of "the other." They take their interrogation of a vacuum cleaner salesman seriously, turning the simplest gesture into a plot against the state. They question Wormold on the nature of a postcard he has written Dr. Hasselbacher on a business trip. Ironically he has thought of the card earlier as a "bad picture of bad hotels with a cross against one window, like the cross in a detective story which indicates where the crime has been committed." With no humor the police ask later:

> "Why have you made a cross on this picture?"
> "It's the window of my room."
> "Why show the window of your room?"
> "Why shouldn't I? It's just—well, it's one of the things one does when traveling."
> "Were you expecting a visitor by the window?"
> "Of course not."
> Who is Dr. Hasselbacher?"
> "An old friend."
> "Is he coming to Santiago?"
> "No!"
> "Then why do you want to show him where your room is?"
> He began to realize what the criminal class knows so well—the impossibility of explaining to a man with power.

He then lies about Dr. Hasselbacher by telling them he is a woman, only to be then accused of being a Protestant and an adulterer. The police really believe the pat calculations of their own detective stories.

This little comic exchange demonstrates the range of the entertainment. Raven cannot find humor in Cholmondeley's sticks of toffee. D is faintly amused at the terrifying country where yellow fog circles around a World War I gas victim while the crowd surges forward to see two pasty princesses shop at Harrod's. Martin's concern for a boyhood friend turned criminal seems sentimental through the cold eyes of detective Calloway in *The Third Man*. But in these novels the direction of tyranny and brutality is fairly well focused. By the time Greene reached *Our Man in Havana* both the political and ethical directions are confused: Wormold seems to be helping the Secret Service guard against a vague "they"— supposedly the Russians—that might establish missile bases on Cuba, but the more present danger seems to be from the fascist dictatorship already established on the island. How seriously can we take ourselves when we have finally been frightened into believing that our enemies would make an ultimate weapon shaped like a giant vacuum cleaner? The fantastic atomic laboratories of Dr. No and Batman tap the very source of those fears. We laugh because there is little use for tears in an age where science has surpassed the ethical imagination.

Greene's entertainments, with their focus on popular literature as a vehicle to portray the complex social situation in an age of radical changes, turn out to be something close to prophetic. Look at the publishing dates: *Stamboul Train* was written in 1932 at the onset of the Third Reich; *Confidential Agent,* the same month Hitler took Poland; *Ministry of Fear* during the blitz; and *Our Man in Havana* a year before Castro's revolution. After the publication of *Ministry of Fear,* Morton Zabel praised Greene's expert evocation of the "familiar phantasm of our age," the "European nightmare" in his entertainments. He notes briefly Greene's indebtedness to slick journalism, films, and mystery stories:

> Every age has its esthetic of crime and horror, its attempts to give form to its special psychic or neurotic climate. No age has imposed greater handicaps on the effort than ours. Crime has gone beyond Addison's "chink in the armor of civilized society; it has become the symptom of a radical leison in the stamina of humanity. The hot violence of the Elizabethans is as different from the cold brutality of Hitlerian Europe. . . .[20]

Greene's thrillers still catch the aesthetic of our age. In a time when the best sellers are "non-fiction novels" about brutal, senseless murders and the last days of a mad Germany, Greene's observation that "thrillers are like life" makes it increasingly difficult to distinguish between melodrama and what we thought was reality.

NOTES

1 Mary McCarthy, "Graham Greene and the Intelligensia," *Partisan Review,* XI (Spring, 1944), 228-30.

2 Francis Kunkel, *The Labyrinthine Ways of Graham Greene* (New York, 1960), p. 58.

3 A. A. de Vitis, "The Entertaining Mr. Greene," *Renascence,* XIV (Fall, 1961), 8-24.

4 David Pryce-Jones, *Graham Greene* (London, 1960), p. 60.

5 Graham Greene, "The Camera Eye," *Spectator,* CLV (1935), 472.

6 John Atkins, "The Curse of the Film," Robert O. Evans (ed.), *Graham Greene: Some Critical Considerations* (Lexington, Ky., 1963), p. 207.

7 Greene, "Subjects and Stories," Charles Davy (ed.), *Footnotes to the Film* (London, 1937), p. 67.

8 Greene, "The Lost Childhood," *The Lost Childhood and Other Essays* (New York, 1951), p. 16.

9 Greene, "Henry James: The Private Universe," *Ibid.,* p. 26.

10 G. K. Chesterton, "A Defence of Detective Stories," Howard Haycroft (ed.), *The Art of the Mystery Story* (New York, 1946), p. 4.

11 Greene, *Journey Without Maps (London,* 1936), p. 10.

12 Greene, "The Revolver in the Corner Cupboard," *The Lost Childhood and Other Essays,* p. 174.

13 Greene, "The Lost Childhood," *Ibid.,* p. 14.

14 Greene's discussion of the bush devil and the witch at the corner occur mostly in *Journey Without Maps,* pp. 219-220, 279.

15 Marjorie Nicholson, "The Professor and the Detective," Aaycroft, p. 118.

16 Greene, "The Lost Childhood," *op. cit.,* p. 15.

17 Harold Gardiner, "Graham Greene, Catholic Shocker," *Renascence* I (Spring, 1949), 13.

18 Charles Brady, "A Melodramatic Cousin of R. L. S.," *America,* LXIV (Jan. 25, 1941), 440.

19 Alistair Cooke, "Epitaph for a Tough Guy," *Atlantic Monthly,* CIC (May, 1957), 33.

20 Morton Zabel, *Craft and Character in Modern Fiction* (New York, 1957), p. 278.

Roger C. Poole

GRAHAM GREENE'S INDIRECTION

This article presents a parallel to my previous article [1] entitled 'Dante's Indirection'. Both are attempts to study a certain method of achieving effects in a reader, a method to which Kierkegaard gave the title 'Indirect Communication'. Both articles are concerned basically with *Kierkegaard's* technique and this perhaps can be clarified by studying indirect methods in other writers. The expression 'Indirect Communication' is ambiguous, as was its use in Kierkegaard's own hands, and sometimes in studying it, in and for itself, one's attention is drawn to parallel and much clearer uses of the principle, when one finds it in poets or novelists of less involved theoretical pretensions. Such a man is Graham Greene, novelist, Catholic, individual. It is to him that I turn for further illustration of the principle which seems to defy (in Kierkegaard's case at least) all attempts at analysis and capture. Critics for over a century, from all countries in the world, have tried to solve the enigma of Kierkegaard's use of Indirect Communication. Perhaps his Indirection can only be approached indirectly. This essay on three novels of Graham Greene is such an attempt.

What did Kierkegaard mean by 'Indirect Communication'? This he sets forth in a book called *The Point of View for My Work as an Author,* a book about which he had such terrible doubts that its publication in complete form was eventually only undertaken by his brother after his death. In it he shows the connection between the 'aesthetic' works and the 'religious' works in his output.

Reprinted by permission of *Blackfriars,* XLV (June, 1964).

His theory is a striking one. The written works are only one half of the 'authorship'. The other half is the 'visual' effect of his own life, which is counterpointed against the works dialectically. The life 'reduplicates' the works.

My contention in this essay, as elsewhere, is that the Indirect Communication in its later phases introduced a category which is of decisive importance, and one which the critics have not evaluated at a methodological level —that I mean of Reduplication. The Danish word is strangely used, as is its English translation, and its best definition is the phrase 'at traede i Karakteer': to step out in character, existentially, to 'exist' something which is believed. Hence the ambivalence of Socrates in Kierkegaard's work, and his famous struggle with Hegel over him: Socrates 'existed' what he believed, and in like manner the category of reduplication comes to include for Kierkegaard the saint and the martyr and, as its highest point, the Imitatio Christi itself.

But as Professor Fabro points out in a perceptive article, [2] the communication of the truth became more and more impossible for Kierkegaard to write out and eventually he solved the whole problem by turning the figure of Christ into incarnate truth, and measuring all earthly efforts and existences by that standard. Christianity at this 'seen' level becomes not so much a script as an existence. It follows from this that there can be no communication in a direct way of the Christian truth.

The *pictorial* effect of the martyr's death, the indirect effect of someone's actions or personality, become then for Kierkegaard the true indirect communication: strangely enough, that is to say, nothing verbal at all. We are playing, as it were, before the darkened hall, in whose darkness we may not pick out any faces we know. Impersonally we are watched, and we act 'in character' as far as we may: we act in character, in order indirectly to have the overwhelming effect on people that such wordless communication can have, to create an artistic effect upon people's moral and spiritual consciousness.

This is a sketch of the effect of the martyr and the saint on the sensibility of their times. It is the effect of the Imitatio Christi. These categories, and their difference from the categories of the genius and the poet, occupied Kierkegaard in the period when he was writing his great love-poems to Christ himself, *The Works of Love* (1847) and *Training in Christianity* (1850). His own analysis of himself becomes acute at this point as never before. In the Journal he writes:

About myself.
Christianity in these parts simply does not exist; but before there can be any question of its being restored again 'first a poet's heart must break, and I am that poet'—these words of mine about myself are only too true . . . Denmark has need of a dead man . . . the God-Man is the only individual who can express Christianity by himself. When it is not the God-Man it always requires at the very least two in order to express Christianity.[3]

'At the very least two in order to express Christianity'. The communicational implications of this are my subject in the rest of this article, as Greene works it out in his Saint and Martyr (the 'whisky-priest' of *The Power and the Glory*) and in three other indirections which cause a conversion or a redefinition. It seems to me that the greatest effect of an indirect communication is that it leads to a redefinition. The three other such cases I want particularly to look at are the conversion of Sarah in *The End of the Affair;* the consequent process of being profoundly moved, which happens to Bendrix her lover; and finally the deep understanding which comes to Scobie in *The Heart of the Matter* when he stares upon the dead body of Ali.

All four places (there are many others) are famous already and have their philosophical orientation marvellously done for them in cultural and theological terms by Paul Rostenne.[4] To set these situations in a general cultural pattern and crisis is his concern there, and it could not be done better.

But I am only concerned with these passages insofar as they illuminate my especial theme, the way, that is, that to 'step out in character', or to reduplicate something believed, is to have colossal effects on others, perhaps effects which reach down to the deepest levels of their unconscious need for faith and lead them insensibly or violently to it.

Kierkegaard's vision of the martyr as the ultimate Christian achievement is given pure expression in *The Power and the Glory,* where the whisky-priest is on the run. On p. 210 [5] we have the morning of the whisky-priest's death:

Tears poured down his face; he was not at the moment afraid of damnation—even the fear of pain was in the background. He felt only an immense disappointment because he had to go to God empty-handed, with nothing at all. It seemed to him, at that moment, that it would have been quite easy to have been a saint. It would only have needed a little self-restraint and a little courage. He felt like someone who has missed happiness by seconds at an appointed place. He knew now that at the end there was only one thing that counted—to be a saint.

It may seem as if Greene has reached the extreme point of pathos here, as if the God-Man (to use Kierkegaard's paradox in reverse direction) were truly so insignificant that one might not notice his achieved state of Reduplication. The paradox is in reverse direction, for of course, for Kierkegaard, the absolute Paradox is that God should be incarnated for an historical moment in Man. For Greene, the absolute Paradox is that Man should for a moment in history be incarnated in God. For that is Greene's meaning here. The little whisky-priest takes on the quality of the divine and can bless others precisely because of the quality of his humility and his doubt. At his execution the priest, who is torn with remorse that he has achieved nothing of spiritual greatness, that he is not even worthy of Hell, inspires the Lieutenant (p. 201), Mr. Tench (p. 216) and the nameless family who read the lives of the martyrs (pp. 217-222) to acknowledge that here indeed was a saint and a martyr, and, by so inspiring them, brings back to their secular and desiccated consciousnesses an impression of spiritual greatness and possibility, indirectly moving them, perhaps at an unconscious level, to a greater spiritual moment in themselves.

There is a moment in the actual execution of the priest when the analogy to the crucified Christ is very clear. When Mr. Tench observes the execution from his window, he seems to hear the whisky-priest cry out the word 'Excuse':

> The officer stepped aside, the rifles went up, and the little man suddenly made jerky movements with his arms. He was trying to say something... but perhaps his mouth was too dry, because nothing came out except a word that sounded like 'Excuse'...

The reference is surely to 'Father, forgive them; for they know not what they do'. The Imitatio Christi has been fearlessly carried to its highest point. Its indirection in terms of Reduplication is at the point of snapping.

We come then to the second of the three cases I have selected of Indirect Communication, in this case between Sarah in *The End of the Affair,* and a crucifix in a Roman Catholic church she happens to enter. The hidden nature of the divinity wells out of the piece, enriching and answering to some deepest pattern in Sarah towards which she is obscurely struggling.

> When I came in and sat down and looked round I realised it was a Roman church, full of plaster statues and bad art. I hated the statues, the crucifix, all the emphasis on the human body. I was trying to escape from the human body and all it needed. I thought I could believe in some kind of a God that bore no relation to ourselves, something vague, amorphous, cosmic... I thought, instead of my own body, of Maurice's ... I thought of a new scar on his shoulder... and I knew I wanted that scar to exist through all eternity.... So today I

looked at that material body on that maerial cross, and I wondered, how could the world have nailed a vapour there? A vapour of course felt no pain and no pleasure. . . . Suppose God did exist, suppose he was a body like that, what's wrong in believing that his body existed as much as mine? (p. 107-110).

Sarah is indirectly touched by an image of something physical, and takes its inner significance to herself by unwilingly and angrily dipping her physical hand into the water, the spiritual effect of which is healing and faith. She sees here that indirectly she is becoming convinced that her previous rationalisations against Smythe were mere lack of attention to detail and to real experience or thought. The path to faith lies through another human being, Maurice, and through his body: we are reprehensible before the bar of complete human sensibility if we bring so little, as we usually do, of our emotional and intellectual abilities to bear on what God means. Here Sarah feels the physical and emotional need of God for her complete being (at whatever depth the unconscious is involved in Jung's terms) and feels God move uneasily on the cross in response to the urgency of her projected desire. The Indirection moves Sarah to redefinition in this way, that she sees there is nothing to be gained by dividing God off from the whole range of her physical and emotional sensibilities, from some deep region of which, doubtless, the intense need for faith arises in its first instance.

Sarah however is in a very receptive state to such impressions. She has been keeping the Diary, the Diary as it falls into Bendrix's hand is to have the indirect effect on him that Sarah's contagious love of God has for everyone. We see in these Diary entries the superb structuring of the novel as an indirect piece. On the 10th January 1946 Sarah writes:

tonight the rain soaked through my coat and my clothes and into my skin, and I shivered with the cold, and it was for the first time as though I nearly loved You. I walked under Your windows in the rain and I wanted to wait under them all night only to show that after all I might learn to love and I wasn't afraid of the desert any longer because You were there... (p. 111).

We remark the extraordinarily subtle use of capital and small letters in the word 'You'. We understand 'it was for the first time as though I nearly loved You' as an expression for God, but we are confounded when the capital is retained for 'Your windows' when the subject is evidently Bendrix. Likewise 'I wasn't afraid of the desert any longer because You were there' maintains the obscurity in Sarah's mind about whether she is thinking of Bendrix as divine or of God as human. Again we have the Kierkegaardian Paradox of Incarnation in reverse direction. On page 120 Sarah begins a love-letter to 'You', where God is directly addressed, but the confusion between God's body on the crucifix and Bendrix's body is still maintained deliberately by Greene:

I have no need to write to You or to talk to You, that's how I began a letter to You a little time ago, and I was ashamed of myself and I tore it up... did I ever love Maurice as much before I loved You? Or was it really You I loved all the time? Did I touch You when I touched him?... But was it me he loved, or You? For he hated in me the things You hate. He was on Your side all the time without knowing it...

Here again we meet the psychological issues slantingly. Bendrix is represented as being potentially a lover of God. It is through women that the redemption is worked so richly and so many times in Greene's novels, which is in keeping with the most sensitive theories of the unconscious and its salvation by the pattern of the *Anima*. Sarah's Diary however goes on to pray for Bendrix, and in a way which will catch at Bendrix's heart when he reads it. Sarah, in contact with the divine in herself, knowing herself now utterly as God's thing (through her body) can look down on Bendrix as from a superior height in human achievement, from the indirect position of the Saint:

But even the first time, in the hotel near Paddington, we spent all we had. You were there teaching us to squander. Like You taught the rich man, so that one day we might have nothing left except this love of You. But You are too good to me. When I ask You for pain, You give me peace. Give it him too. Give him my peace—he needs it more.

'Give him my peace'. The implications of spiritual bounty are too plain to ignore. Whether or not we are to accept Greene's account of her childhood baptism as decisive in this later fullness, we see that something has led Sarah to this profound richness of being. Sarah has 'miraculous' effects on several other people in the book, when like Kierkegaard she is become 'in the most solemn sense of the word, an "absent one".' I do not think it relevant to discuss here whether this is a formal effect of baptism. Greene presents it to us as the experience of someone who knows herself deeply enough, even at the unconscious level, to give peace and grace to others. She is moved by her *Animus* to understand the *whole* of her spiritual longing. Indirectly then, by this prayer for the soul of Bendrix (who 'needs peace more') she answers to his search for the *Anima*. Psychologically the structure is complete.

We come now to the criterion to 'suffer for' as opposed to simple suffering. To 'suffer for' is peculiar to Greene's characters, who find their eventual release from their own suffering in feeling more for someone else. This is true of the whisky-priest with his daughter, as it is of Querry in *A Burnt-Out Case* and Scobie in *The Heart of the Matter*. Here Sarah 'suffers for' Bendrix. This defines the quality of her faith and makes possible for Bendrix in terms of peace and love a redefinition of what faith might mean. In a sense, the thought is 'He prayeth best who loveth best'. To pray for the peace of someone else's soul is surely to pray from an answering quality in one's own. If then one feels the presence and pain of another in a prayer, so that it is a real extension of one's own, then the prayer offered up on his or her behalf is equally offered up on one's own behalf. Everything becomes extension in the act of prayer and by praying for peace in another, one receives it in intense form in oneself.

At this point our third Indirection may be introduced. Sarah's spiritual understanding does not stream out into the void and waste itself. It achieves a series of indirect results which are the definition of her faith and the re-definition of Bendrix's and others'.

We remember how Bendrix reads the Diary, and is struck by her 'leap' and the ensuing sense of peace:

> ... If this God exists, I thought, and if even you—with your lusts and adulteries and the timid lies you used to tell—can change like this, we could all be saints by leaping as you leapt, by shutting the eyes and leaping once and for all: if *you* are a saint, it's not so difficult to be a saint. It's something He can demand of any of us, leap'. (p. 186).

We are precisely in the area of the Kierkegaardian 'leap of faith'. No better definition of his meaning could be given than this reaction in Bendrix.

Bendrix is in the very condition of susceptibility, the state which Kierkegaard in *The Sickness Unto Death* characterises as 'being unconsciously in despair'. Kierkegaard in a Journal entry from the same period has characterised this state brilliantly:

> There is only one proof of the truth of Christianity and that, quite rightly, is from the emotions, when the dread of sin and a heavy conscience torture a man into crossing the narrow line between despair bordering upon madness—and Christianity. *There* lies Christianity! [6]

If this is not orthodox, we need only note it and pass on: it is the kind of argument that appeals to unorthodox men of passionate natures like Kierkegaard, and here Bendrix. For Greene there is nothing worse than the pat orthodox answer to the involved emotional processes of the individual who is struggling to find his wholeness. Bendrix is stung by his feeling of being robbed of Sarah by God into these words:

But I won't leap. I sat on my bed and said to God: You've taken her, but You haven't got me yet. . . . You're a devil, God, tempting us to leap. But I don't want Your peace and I don't want Your love. I wanted something very simple and very easy: I wanted Sarah for a lifetime and You took her away . . . I hate You, God, I hate You as though You existed. (p. 186).

The protestation is too violent for credence. And we remember Sarah's conviction that hate no less than love is a proof of the existence of God:

I thought, sometimes I've hated Maurice, but would I have hated him if I hadn't loved him too? Oh God, if I could really hate you, what would that mean? (p. 110).

We see what it means in the tortured doubt of Bendrix as the book closes. He has to make the decision that Kierkegaard sketched out, the real Either/Or when times become more than one can bear: despair bordering upon madness—or Christianity.

But Sarah was convinced against her conscious will, by the Indirection of a crucifix. Bendrix is convinced against his conscious will by her Diary. Sarah, by making a present of her reaction to the crucifix and by bothering to record that experience in her Diary, leaves open the path to her experience through the only mode that she and Bendrix have in common—the body and the memory of physical love. Thus Bendrix cannot fight rationally what he reads in her Diary, because it was not with the rational part of her that Sarah felt the need for faith but with the body, which by then was an analogy to Bendrix's body. Thus Sarah's conversion, couched as it is in the terms which most concerned Bendrix, 'takes' on Bendrix and he falls inevitably sick of the same longing and the same need. Greene has elsewhere characterised faith as a virus in the bloodstream.

We turn lastly to Scobie in *The Heart of the Matter*. Scobie's desperate search is for peace.

. . . He dreamed of peace day and night . . peace seemed to him the most beautiful word in the language: My peace I give you, my peace I leave with you: O Lamb of God, who takest away the sins of the world, grant us thy peace. In the Mass he pressed his fingers against his eyes to keep the tears of longing in (p. 58).

Scobie is another example, like Sarah, of how God breaks into an already God-permeated consciousness, which stands on the verge of identifying itself. When Scobie at the end of the novel stares down on the body of his servant Ali, to whose murder he is party, he is overwhelmed by a rush of love for his fellow creature's body, just as Sarah had been by the crucifix. The crucifix image is again present, and it is Ali's body which moves Scobie's soul to the freeing love that has always escaped him, the lack of which is his passionate longing for peace:

The body lay coiled and unimportant like a broken watch-spring under a pile of empty drums . . . for a moment he saw the body as something very small and dark and a long way away—like a broken piece of the rosary he looked for: a couple of black beads and the image of God coiled at the end of it. Oh God, he thought, I've killed you: you've served me all these years and I've killed you at the end of them. God lay there under the petrol drums and Scobie felt the tears in his mouth, salt in the cracks of his lips. You served me and I did this to you. You were faithful to me, and I wouldn't trust you. 'What is it, sah?' the corporal whispered, kneeling by the body. 'I loved him', Scobie said (p. 238).

The 'corporal' kneeling by the body we may see as the physical raised to the level of personification in Scobie's mind—and the symbolic value of kneeling shows how highly Scobie now values the spirit as represented by the body—the body cast away, disowning him. We have here another re-enactment of the Passion of Christ as we did in the case of the whisky-priest's death: the suffering servant, betrayed first and then killed by those he served, by those he loved and by those he trusted. As with Kierkegaard, there is a Christology here of the Suffering Servant, the humble lover, the cast-off redeemer, and Greene embodies it in his whisky-priest and his Ali, where Kierkegaard dwells long, in the book called *Training in Christianity,* on the humble Inviter, whose invitation is universal, Come unto me . . .

> Ali's body, the body of the servant who was trustworthy, had cast him off, disowned him—'I know you not'. He swore aloud, hysterically. 'By God, I'll get the man who did this', but under that anonymous stare insincerity withered. He thought: I am the man (p. 238).

Here in the phrase 'I am the man' we have the overtones of 'Ecce Homo', and of Peter's denial in the Courtyard, 'I know not the man', as well as Nathan's 'Thou art the man'. It is noticeable too that Scobie cries, like Peter, hysterically and afterwards weeps just as bitterly. The denial is done, for ever. Ali alive was a mixture of spirit and body. Scobie had perhaps never really thought about Ali's body, because he was the servant, the tactfully absent. But when one is in the presence of death, when there is no longer the spirit, then the injury to the spirit of the deceased is figured forth by the presence of the body left behind on the shore of life. As Sarah discovered, if God were a mere 'vapour' one could not love him. Here 'God lay there under the petrol drums'. He is body, killed like that figure hanging in 'imaginary pain' on its wooden cross, and by its finality, with powerful Indirection, moving the viewer to redefine his beliefs, to redefine himself, before the final act of Reduplication.

Scobie, like Sarah, discovers the difference between suffering and 'suffering for'. With the 'suffering for' Ali, Scobie is released into love. Before the body, he feels neither grief nor remorse. These (for Scobie conventional) responses are switched off. Scobie feels only the overwhelming love of 'suffering for'.

The Indirection in this fourth case, of the human body of Ali, causes a redefinition. It springs out pictorially, in the simplest of things, very often in the human body as emblem for a personality, but it is the revelation of what that body stood for, what that death stood for, what that act stood for, what that love stood for, which is the essential revelation of the hidden nature of the divine in man, and of man in the divine. It is this sense of revelation which is at the core of the theology both of Greene and of Kierkegaard. I use 'revelation' not as a term of glory, of theological grandeur on which tomes have been written, but in a real sense as the revelation of everyday things in their infinite preciousness, and this includes human love as its apex. This is what the revelation of God is like for Greene and for Kierkegaard, as if, standing back, we *see* for the first time what it was we possessed, how precious it was, that we mishandled it, that we despised it, that maybe we even killed it, and then we see in what sense it is true for both writers that, in the words of the whisky-priest:

> Loving God isn't any different from loving a man—or a child. It's wanting to be with Him, to be near Him. . . . It's wanting to protect Him from yourself. (p. 173).

Earlier in the book (p. 102) the whisky-priest had meditated that:

> If God had been like a toad, you could have rid the globe of toads, but when God was like yourself, it was no good being content with stone figures—you had to kill yourself among the graves.

It is my contention that, in a similar way, the sense of the human in the divine and the divine in the human, both for Kierkegaard and for Greene, is brought about by the indirect means of outward objects and the relations we have to other human beings. The martyr and the saint and the Imitatio Christi are all good solid orthodox concepts—but it is against their being taken in an orthodox way that Greene struggles so hard. Greene uses the Christian types and pictures, but in a hidden, subtle, new, indirect way. He incarnates states and attributes: by doing so he makes us, his readers, reckon with things which we may have committed mentally to the theologian and the back shelf of the public library. Greene recognises that these types, the saint, the martyr and the Imitatio Christi are in fact people we meet every day, only we are too theoretical and too obvious-minded to look closely enough to see the divinity shining through. He also suggests that these types bring us spiritual health and peace—Greene is a psychologist, and knows that human beings are in constant search for those religious forms which answer to the requirements of their deepest spiritual and emotional forces. These hungers, one might call them, for the hero and the saint and the Christ, may be characterised (to borrow Jung's terminology for a moment) as hungers for the Symbols of the Self. What the force of the word 'Symbol' is in Jung's phrase I do not feel able to define, but some such profound search is going on in the heart and unconscious of everyone who is not a spiritual cretin. It is to these people, 'moving about in worlds not realised', that Greene addresses his types and his paradoxical seekers. Thus while the Jungian analysis of religion has its validity, Greene insists that the types and symbols of the Christian religion are to be met much more really in human life than they are in human dreams and neuroses. *Types in dreams represent a wished-for wholeness. Types in human everyday life represent achieved wholeness.* Types in conscious life are therefore the higher form, as the actual is over the potential. Whatever the low psychological parentage of faith, it is in its acceptance crowned like a king. It may start from the lowest and most abject needs of the human heart, but may finally achieve the beauty of a transcendent moment when that faith may be existentially realised in an act: which reduplicates what is believed to be the good and the true. Kierkegaard warns us against any man who claims to love God for any other reason than that he needs God desperately[7] and this may be understood psychologically too in Jungian terms. For Jung, support and healing come from the least likely place of all, from the Self; hence, he says, [8] 'the archetype of the lowly origin of the Redeemer'. Kierkegaard's love poem to the figure of Christ as we have it in *Training in Christianity* shows us such a Redeemer, poor, lonely, despised and rejected. He is so like oneself, that his invitation, 'Come unto me all ye that labour', coming from such an unlikely quarter, almost makes one overlook the fact that this Inviter is the source of all spiritual peace and rest. 'It is not time', asks Jung in *The Undiscovered Self*, 'that the Christian mythology, instead of being wiped out, was understood symbolically for once?' And again of modern man he asks, 'Does he know that he is on the point of losing the life-preserving myth of the inner man which Christianity has treasured up for him? Does he realise what lies in store should this catastrophe ever befall him?' The Indirection in Kierkegaard's own view of the martyr, who must be first and foremost 'reflective' in the modern age, as of the saint and of the Imitatio Christi, *implicates* the observer. Such I believe is the intention and practice of Graham Greene. As novelist he aims at some such result. If for Greene human actions can approximate to an analogy of the divine then certainly for Kierkegaard the divine may look so human as to defeat the eye.

To those people today who are concerned to evaluate relative claims of theology and philosophy and psychology, it seems to me that this kind of indirect study of very different writers sometimes manages to destroy *parti pris* very usefully. Like Bultmann and Bonhoeffer, for example, Greene is concerned with essences. But unlike them he does not believe that these essences are communicable without forms and symbols, without Indirection and without pictorial, reduplicated, significance. In redefining some aspects of faith as relations between 'You' and 'you' (the 'two at the very least' of Kierkegaard) Greene uses every shade from his palette. He is psychologist and lover. Like Kierkegaard, Greene, even when he is analysing man, still loves him. When he forces his characters to think, he forces them at the same time to feel, and this may account for the extraordinary veracity of the experience of conversion or redefinition which we get in one after another of Greene's novels.

NOTES

1 *Blackfriars* (April, 1963).
2 Fabro, "La communicazione della verità nel pensiero di Kierkegaard," *Studi Kierkegaardiani* (Brescia, 1957).
3 Journal X 4, A. 586, Dru's translation No. 1258.
4 Paul Rostenne, *Graham Greene: témoin des temps tragiques* (Paris, 1949).
5 I refer to the Penguin editions throughout this article.
6 Journal X I A. 467, Dru's translation No. 926.
7 Soren Kierkegaard, *Christian Discourses,* translated by W. Lowrie, (London, 1939), p. 198.
8 C. G. Jung, *Psychology and Alchemy* (*Collected Works* edited by H. Read and others and translated by R. F. C. Hull, Vol. XII [Princeton]), p. 28.

R. W. B. Lewis

THE 'TRILOGY' OF GRAHAM GREENE[1]

For: K571
What bore / tore;
the horror and the glory are the same.
—R. P. Blackmur, "The Rape of Europa"

In Graham Greene's early fiction, along with a definite but notably uneven development of style and vigor, there was an apparent failure to distinguish between various fictional genres. Even *Brighton Rock* betrays an initial confusion between what Greene calls an "entertainment" and what he finally offered as a tragedy; but here the confusion is unexpectedly exploited (as shall be seen) in the composition of an immensely impressive novel. The distinction of genres, in a somewhat Gallic manner, would become important for Greene, and in a sense the making of him; but prior to *Brighton Rock*, we observe an uncertainty of artistic purpose which led to an unstable treatment of the basic elements of fiction: setting, character and action. Part of the success of *Brighton Rock, The Power and the Glory* and *The Heart of the Matter* is due to the preliminary sketching of elements in each of them —a process which, as it turned out, managed to release the special energy and "vision" which would characterize Greene as a writer of stature.

The settings of *The Power and the Glory* and *The Heart of the Matter*, for example, had already been explored by Greene personally and in two excellent travel-books: *The*

Reprinted by permission of *Modern Fiction Studies,* III (Autumn, 1957).

Lawless Roads, from which whole passages are transcribed in the former; and *Journey Without Maps,* which concludes on the Gold Coast of poor Major Scobie. In the travel-books, Greene's journalistic and photographic abilities exhausted themselves; and in the novels, consequently, physical settings could be managed so as to exude a meaning which in fact transformed them into spiritual situations, into elaborated images of fate. Mexico, however discolored, is still Mexico in *The Lawless Roads;* in *The Power and the Glory,* it has been reduced and reshaped to fit a particular action, of which indeed it contains the particular secret. Similarly, each member of the "trilogy" has its correlative entertainment: mystery stories in the popular sense which function ably as trial-runs for mystery dramas in a more ancient and theological sense. Here we touch the crucial distinction underlying the other distinctions, for the mystery of the human condition, beyond or beneath any sociological or historical or psychological explanation thereof, has become Greene's obsessive subject. Raven, the killer in *A Gun for Sale,* with his dumb conviction of injustice and his bleak yearning for a soul he can trust, is a purely human cartoon for the metaphysical monster, Pinkie, the killer of *Brighton Rock.* In *The Confidential Agent,* the weary and frightened fidelity to his mission of the Spanish agent, D., is a sketchy and political version of the behavior of the nameless Mexican priest, the agent of God, on his exclusively religious mission in *The Power and the Glory.* And *The Ministry of Fear,* the most skillful of the entertainments and a very good story indeed, dramatizes what Greene regards as the most dangerous of human emotions, pity, the fatal flaw which would destroy Major Scobie in *The Heart of the Matter,* but which is significantly contrasted in that novel with its real opposite, the primary attribute of God: mercy.

It can be said about the earlier novels, then, that the relative and diminishing confusion of purpose, and the blurry handling of the elements, are rooted in a failure to disentangle the *mystery* of the mystery, to separate it out from the contingencies of melodrama and the staged surprises of the brain-twister. The disentanglement followed, as it seems, upon the Liberian experience examined above; for after that, the plot and the action of Greene's novels are increasingly given their meaning by the religious motif—a motif which, since it cannot always be called Christian, can scarcely be always called Catholic; a sort of shocked intuition of supernature. It is when the religious motif takes charge that Greene's resources—including his nervous, highly pressured style, and his uncommon talent for narrative—become ordered and controlled, and his very real artistic power fulfills itself.[2] *The Man Within* has an appealing youthfulness of viewpoint; but the religious element remains shadowy and generalized, and the whole story wobbles uneasily to (in context) a rather pointless climax. The real source of complexity in human events, as Greene would eventually see it, is not detected in *The Name of Action,* though that is what the novel is about; as a result, we are introduced here only to shapeless movements in a nightmare world. And in *England Made Me,* which is otherwise a genuine achievement, Greene so far misunderstood himself as to insert stream-of-consciousness meditations ill-advisedly but patently borrowed from James Joyce. Nothing could be further from Greene's intentions than those of Joyce—the careful rendering of the behavior of the mind, with the ultimate aim of celebrating the shaping power of art, the "stasis" which imposes value and meaning upon the chaos of mental experience. What Greene has envisaged and what he has become especially concerned with are better implied in the title of still another early book, *It's A Battlefield*: the human scene now described as a battlefield between transcendent warring forces. Greene has never reverted to the Joycian technique.[3] And in *Brighton Rock,* the metaphor of the battlefield is dominant: "It lay there always, the ravaged and disputed territory between the two eternities."

The three novels published between 1938 and 1948 are sometimes taken together as a trilogy; but the word should be surrounded by quotation marks, for the trilogistic pattern, if any, took hold only belatedly. But it is worth juxtaposing the three books, to observe several striking aspects of Greene. All three show Greene's affection for the primitive; like Ignazio Silone, Greene often turns away from the relatively civilized to inspect human life in its cruder and more exposed conditions: a dark constricted corner of Brighton, the jungles and the prisons of Tabasco, the coast of West Africa—all places where, as Scobie tells himself in *The Heart of the Matter,* "human nature hasn't had time to disguise itself"; places where there openly flourished "the injustices, the cruelties, the meanness that elsewhere people so cleverly hushed up." Upon these primitive scenes, we encounter the *dramatis personae* of Greene's recurring drama and of his troubled universe: the murderer, the priest and the policeman, who are the heroes respectively of the three books. All three figures appear in all three novels; and they tend more and more to resemble each other. The murderer, Pinkie, is knowingly a spoiled, a hideously inverted priest; the policeman, Scobie, becomes involved with crime and criminals; the officer in *The Power and the Glory* has "something of a priest in his intent observant walk," while the priest in turn has queer points of resemblance with the Yankee killer whose photograph faces his in the police station. The three figures represent, of course, the shifting and the interwoven attributes of Greenian man: a being capable of imitating both Christ and Judas; a person who is at once the pursuer and the man pursued; a creature with the splendid potentiality either of damnation or salvation. The actualities of their fate exhaust, apparently, the major possibilities. If one can be sure of anything in the real world or in Greene's world, Pinkie Brown is damned—it is his special mode of triumph; the Mexican priest is saved —sainthood gleams at last through his bloodshot eyes; and the final end of Major Scobie is what is precisely in doubt, as difficult to determine as his own ambiguous last words, "Dear God, I love . . ." Pinkie is a proud citizen of hell; Scobie's suffering is that of a man in purgatory; and the laughter in *The Power and the Glory* celebrates, perhaps, the entrance of a soul into paradise. The three careers are presented to us in three very different kinds of fiction; *Brighton Rock* just manages to escape melodrama and becomes a work *sui generis; The Power and the Glory* is, in its way, a divine comedy; and *The Heart of the Matter* is a tragedy in the classical tradition. These novels are, respectively, Greene's most strenuous, his most satisfying, and, artistically, his most assured.

I

Brighton Rock in particular is the most harrowing of Greene's stories about children; and Pinkie, the seventeen-year-old gangster (he is usually referred to simply as "the Boy"), is "the most driven and 'damned'" of all Greene's characters, to quote his own words about the evil forces in that other fearful children's tale, James's *The Turn of the Screw*. There is, to be sure, a superficial movement in the novel from death to life: the narrative begins with the revenge-murder by Brighton race-track hoodlums of the man, Hale, who is working a publicity stunt for a newspaper among the holiday crowds; and it closes with the pregnancy of Rose, the wan, under-age wife whom Hale's killer, Pinkie, has been forced for protection to marry. Here, insofar, is a momentary likeness with Moravia's *Woman of Rome,* which similarly, concludes with the heroine's pregnancy by a now dead murderer and which does so quite definitely to suggest the painful victory of life over death. But Greene's artistic and intellectual purposes are almost always dialectically opposite to those of Moravia; and in *Brighton Rock,* not only is the death legally avenged, the birth itself will be altogether darkened by Rose's discovery of Pinkie's true feeling about her—via the "loving message" he has recorded by phonograph, and which, "the worst horror of all," she is on her way to hear as the story ends: "God damn you, you little bitch, why can't you go back home for ever and let me be?" The implied denouncement in *Brighton Rock* is as disagreeable as anything in modern fiction. But *Brighton Rock* is a deliberately pitiless book, and partly because it aims, by moving beyond human pity, to evoke the far, faint light of an incomprehensible divine mercy. It is a pitiless book, with disaster lurking in every syllable.[4]

A portion of the threatened disaster is artistic: a threat to the shape and character of the book itself. Greene evidently began it as an "entertainment," and the first American edition announced itself as such. He began it, that is, as a melodrama of murder and detection in which contingency and coincidence would be allowed free play, the chase be exciting for its own sake, and with a larger and more kindly emphasis than the novel eventually allowed on Ida Arnold, the London lady of easy virtue who had known Hale in his last frightened hours and who sets herself to discover the criminal, an aim she formidably succeeds in. But evil has always stimulated Greene a good deal more than the righting of wrongs; and in this case, the figure and story of Pinkie Brown (unlike those of Raven in *A Gun for Sale,* of which *Brighton Rock* would otherwise have been a repetition) expanded in Greene's imagination until a recognizable tragedy took its place in the book alongside the well-made entertainment.

The entertainment is Ida's; it begins with the first sentence ("Hale knew, before he had been in Brighton three hours, that they meant to murder him"), and ends with the police closing in on the culprit. The tragedy is Pinkie's; *it* begins more subtly in the atmosphere of the place (implied by the adjectives used for the jostling crowds, "bewildered," "determined," "cramped," "closed," "weary"); and its action is defined in advance by the book's motto, from *The Witch of Edmonton,* with overtones of *Macbeth* —"This were a fine reign: / To do ill and not hear of it again." In the open world of the entertainment, happenstances accumulate; but in the tragedy, there is no space for contingency, no time for the accidental. Evil is fertile and is always heard of again; every move Pinkie makes—from the killing of Hale, through further necessitated murders and the detested courtship and marriage, to the climax in which, like Oedipus, he blinds himself (with vitriol)—has a convulsive inevitability, the more dreadful since it seems rooted neither in private temperament nor in social background. It derives from the inexplicable power of evil, one of the two things that Pinkie believes in: *"Credo in unum Satanum." Brighton Rock* confirms Greene's statement in the preface to a book about him by the French critic, Paul Rostenne, that he has no *a priori* edifying purpose in writing his novels, but is carried along rather by the unpredictable energies of his characters. As Pinkie's perils increase and his ambitions enlarge, the very design of the book shifts and re-forms.

The result could have been a kind of disaster: two different books, between the same covers only by mistake. But the actual result is an original and striking work: for the relation between the detective story and the tragedy is exactly what *Brighton Rock* is finally all about. It is a relation between modes of narrative discourse which reflects a relation between two kinds or levels of reality: a relation between incommensurable and hostile forces; between incompatible worlds; between the ethical world of right and wrong, to which Ida constantly and confidently appeals, and the theological world of good and evil inhabited by Pinkie and Rose. It is, in short, the relation Greene had formulated for himself in Liberia, between the "sinless empty graceless chromium world" of modern western urban civilization and the supernaturally infested jungle with its purer terrors and its keener pleasures. The abrupt superiority of *Brighton Rock* to anything Greene had yet written is owing to this, that for the first time he separated the *misterium* from the mystery and confronted the one with the other.

Here, of course, the confrontation takes the form of deadly warfare: "She [Ida] stared out over the red and green lights, the heavy traffic of her battlefield, laying her plans, marshalling her cannon fodder." That sense of the universal drama is both ancient and modern; for *Brighton Rock,* to put the case in perhaps exaggerated and misleading theological terms, belongs with the early and late medieval tradition, the tradition now again in fashion: the tradition of Tertullian and the dark, negative, and incorrigibly paradoxical theology, wherein everything supernatural stands in implacable hostility over against everything natural and human; and for the most part, vice versa. This is the view Albert Camus has identified and attacked as *the* Christian tradition. But in another tradition, in so-called theocentric humanism, there are intermediate ends, intermediate goods and intermediate explanations: because there is an intermediate figure, the God-man Christ, who reconciles the realms and makes sense out of human history. But about Pinkie and his small explosive world, there is nothing intermediate—here everything is sudden and ultimate. Pinkie has no great involvement with the things of this world, with money or with sexual love or even with Brighton. His Brighton is not a town or a "background" but a fury-driven situation; and he is involved immediately with evil and catastrophe.

He is deeply implicated, too, of course, with good—with the forlorn waitress Rose, who has just enough information about Hale's murder to make Pinkie decide savagely to marry her in order to keep her quiet; and who is as doomed to salvation (that is how Greene prefers to describe it) as he is to damnation. He sees her as his necessary counterpart. "What was most evil in him needed her; it couldn't get along without her goodness. . . . Again he got the sense that she completed him." Their world too is a battlefield, but with a difference: "Good and evil lived together in the same country, spoke the same language, came together like old friends, feeling the same completion, touching hands beside the iron bedstead. . . . Their world lay there always, the ravaged and disputed territory between two eternities. They faced each other as it were from opposing territories, but like troops at Christmas time they fraternized."[5] In *Brighton Rock,* the theme of companionship which takes so many forms in the fiction of the second generation appears as the reluctant fellowship between good and evil and is symbolized in the illegal marriage of Pinkie and Rose and the uncertain sexual union of the two virgins on their wedding night. There, touching hands beside the iron bedstead, they peer out together at the "glare and open world," the utterly alien world of Ida Arnold. "She was as far from either of them as she was from Hell—or Heaven."

In Ida's world, the religious impulse is softened and made comfortable; but in Pinkie's world, the human impulse shrivels and looks ugly. Only the most extreme alternatives are offered—not even sacred and profane love, for example, but the supernatural and the obscene. Normal love is reduced to the pornographic, and is opposed only by fidelity to supernature; here, as in *England Made Me,* religion becomes a substitute or almost a heightened form of pornography. Pinkie quotes venomously from the cheap literature, "the kind you buy under the counter. Spicer used to get them. About girls being beaten. Full of shame to expose herself thus before the boys she stooped." But in choosing the alternative, in submitting to the supernatural, Pinkie attaches himself primarily to supernatural evil. *"Credo in unum satanum"* is the violent admission elicited on the same page by the outburst against pornography; and though he tells Rose scornfully, "Of course there's Hell," about Heaven he can only say, "Maybe, maybe."

As Pinkie pursues his dream of damnation, the tragic dimension of *Brighton Rock* turns into a sort of saint's life in reverse. The seven sections of the book dramatize one by one an inversion of all or most of the seven sacraments, dramatise what we might call the seven deadly sacraments: [6] as Pinkie is confirmed in the habit of murder ("Hell lay about him in his infancy. He was ready for more death"), is ordained as a priest of his satanic church ("When I was a kid, I swore I'd be a priest. . . . What's wrong with being a priest? They know what's what"), performs the act of matrimony which here is a mortal sin, and receives the vitriolic unction in the moment of his death. The entire reversal accomplished in *Brighton Rock,* haphazard though it is, manages to dignify the repellent protagonist on the principle indicated to Rose, at the very end, by the sniffling old priest: *Corruptio optimi est pessima.* The worst is the corruption of the best; only the potentially very good can become so very evil, and only the sacraments which save can so effectively become the sacraments which blast.

Despite its singularly uninviting character, accordingly, the narrow and oppressive world of Pinkie Brown is clearly to be honored—in the terms of the novel—over the spiritual bourgeoisie of Ida Arnold. Her world, for all its robust good humor, is increasingly represented as sterile, and she as a hollow, heartless menace. Ida, with her big breasts and her warm enveloping body, remains childless; it is the angular, nearly sexless Rose who conceives at once, after a single sexual venture. And the final worldly victory of Ida, her destruction of Pinkie, coincides with a hidden defeat of her own world: a repudiation of it, accomplished relentlessly by the rhetoric of the book. That rhetoric aims at separating out and then destroying the ethical domain, in the name of the theological; the conventional values of right and wrong are lured into prominence and then annihiliated. This is done by a series of oxymorons, or seeming contradictions, which sometimes appear as strained and perverse but often arresting similes. The latter are associated mostly with Pinkie—"his virginity straightened in him like sex"—and suggest the colliding opposites which animate his experience. The oxymorons are employed in the account of Ida and her behavior, and with the intention of transforming or "transvaluating" our judgment of her. When allusion is made to Ida's "remorseless optimism" or her "merciless compassion," the aim is to negate the familiar human attributes—in this case, cheerfulness and pity—by stressing their remoteness from the religious virtues: in this case, penitent humility and mercy. The adjective, from its higher plane, denies all value to the nouns on their lower human level. And the whole process culminates in the epilogue when the priest, coughing and whistling through the grill in that unattractive and seedy way Greene's priests almost always have, says to Rose about Pinkie—destroyed now by the ferocious pity of Ida Arnold—that no human being can conceive "the appalling strangeness of the mercy of God."

About this stylistic technique, which may best be defined as a technique of befuddlement and concerning which one has the uneasy suspicion of mere cleverness, there will be more to say. Meanwhile, it is to be noted that as the detective story and the tragedy intertwine in *Brighton Rock,* we find ourselves in a universe wherein seeming opposites—good and evil—become closely allied, and seeming likenesses—the right and the good—are totally opposed. These paradoxes, too, are incarnate in the central figure. Pinkie, Greene's first memorable image of the character he had so cherished as a boy in *The Viper of Milan*—"perfect evil walking the world where perfect good can never walk again"—is a replica of Judas who has nonetheless faint confusing echoes about him of the perfectly good, of Christ. He is the worst *only* by virtue of being the corruption of the best. And so, when his unstable associate Cubitt is talking about him to Ida and when Cubitt denies being a friend of his—" 'You a friend of Pinkie's?' Ida Arnold asked. 'Christ, no,' Cubitt said and took some more whiskey"—there is the fleeting whisper of a memory: "A courtyard, a sewing wench beside the fire, the cock crowing." And Cubitt goes on to deny him thrice.

Greene never tires of quoting the lines from AE's poem, "Germinal"—

In ancient shadows and twilights
Where childhood had strayed,
The world's great sorrows were born
And its heroes were made.
In the lost boyhood of Judas
Christ was betrayed.

It is not only the realm of supernatural good and its unlikely representative Rose who are betrayed by the lost boyhood of this demonic Judas; it is also the flickers of the Christ in himself. It is within such a context and by such insinuations that Greene earns Pinkie the right to be regarded, as though reflected in a crazy-mirror on Brighton pier, as an image of the tragic hero. There can be no doubt, finally, about the damnation of Pinkie Brown: except the enormous doubt that, according to Greene, must attend our every human judgment and prediction.

II

The motto of *The Power and the Glory* is from Dryden: "Th' inclosure narrow'd; the sagacious power / Of hounds and death drew nearer every hour." The lines could apply to *Brighton Rock* and with a little stretching to *The Man Within,* as well as to most of Greene's entertainments; they summarize Greene's settled view of human experience. But they are peculiarly appropriate to *The Power and the Glory,* which is, one could say, Greene's most peculiarly appropriate novel and which comprises the adventures of a hunted man—the last Catholic priest in a totalitarian Mexican state—whom the hounds of power catch up with and to whom death does come by a firing-squad in the next-to-last chapter of the book. There is no complication of genres here: the novel has a single hero and a single action—and both are luminously representative of the special kind of hero and heroic adventure which characterize the fiction of the second generation.

According to the laws of the new godless state, the priest is an outlaw simply because he carries on his priestly duties; but he has also broken several of the laws of his church. He is a rogue, a *picaro,* in several kinds of ways; his contradictory character includes much of the comical unpredictability of the traditional *picaro;* and the narrative Greene has written about him is perhaps the most patently picaresque of any we are considering—the lively story of the rogue on his travels, or better on his undignified flights from and towards the forces of destruction. In no other novel of the time, moreover, are the paradoxes of sainthood more expertly handled. The priest—who is a slovenly drunkard and the father of a devilish little child; who giggles a good deal and is often helplessly weak at the knees—is also a potential, perhaps finally an actual saint. He feels at the end that he has failed: "It seemed to him, at that moment, that it would have been quite easy to have been a saint. . . . He felt like someone who has missed happiness at an appointed place." But other evidence throughout the book suggests that all unwittingly he had kept his appointment with beatitude. *The Power and the Glory* stands very close beside Silone's *Bread and Wine.* And the so-called "whisky-priest," disguised as a layman and fumbling his way towards disaster, is, if not the twin, at least the younger brother of Pietro Spina, a layman (a revolutionist) disguised as a priest who is similarly the last lonely witness to truth in his own neighborhood, who is equally pursued by the forces of oppression and who is likewise the attractive, incompetent and saintly source of damage and of death to almost everyone involved with him. These two novels give the most revealing account in their generation of the hero as outlaw, fleeing and transcending the various inhuman forms which power currently assumes.

In terms of Greene's artistic and intellectual development, however, another suitable motto might be drawn from the book itself: when the priest, heading bumpily into the hills of Tabasco on mule-back, day-dreams in the imagery of a "simplified mythology"—"Michael dressed in armour slew the dragon, and the angels fell through space like comets with beautiful streaming hair because they were jealous, so one of the Fathers had said, of what God intended for men—the enormous privilege of life—this life." *This life.* In this novel, by a refreshing contrast with *England Made Me* and *Brighton Rock,* the religious impulse no longer denigrates and undermines the human but serves rather to find in it or to introduce into it a kind of beauty and a kind of goodness. "I tell you that heaven is here," the priest cries out to the vacant-faced peasants gathered dumbly in a hut on the mountain-side at dawn. It is, of course, characteristic of Greene that, in *The Power and the Glory,* where the divine image for once irradiates and redeems the human, it is seen doing so only to the most squalid, repellent and pain-wracked of human conditions—just as omens of sanctity are seen only in an unshaven brandy-bibber. Natural beauty is not enhanced, but natural ugliness is touched by grace; for what nauseated Minty in *England Made Me*—the notion of God incarnate [7]—is just what most exhilarates the priest.

> At the centre of his own faith there always stood the convincing mystery— that we are made in God's image—God was the parent, but He was also the policeman, the criminal, the priest, the maniac and the judge. Something resembling God dangled from the gibbet or went into odd attitudes before the bullets in a prison yard or contorted itself like a camel in the attitude of sex. He would sit in the confessional and hear the complicated ingenuities which God's image had thought out: and God's image shook now, up and down on the mule's back, with the yellow teeth sticking out over the lower lip, and God's image did its despairing act of rebellion with Maria in the hut among the rats.

Characteristically, too, it is less the splendor than the almost ridiculous *mystery* of the thing that Greene wants to dramatize. But let him do so in his own manner: in *The Power and the Glory* a compassionate and ultimately a very charitable manner. For it is by seeking God and by finding Him in the darkness and stench of prisons, among the sinners and the rats and the rascals, that the whisky-priest arrives at the richest emotion second-generation fiction has to offer: the feeling of companionship, and especially the companionship of the commonly guilty and wretched. Arrested for carrying brandy, crowded into a pitch-black cell, crushed between unseen odorous bodies, with a woman on one side hysterically demanding to make her trivial confession and an unseen couple copulating somewhere on the floor, announcing their orgasms with whimpering cries of pleasure, the priest is touched suddenly "by an extraordinary affection. He was just one criminal among a herd of criminals . . . he had a sense of companionship which he had never experienced in the old days when pious people came kissing his black cotton glove."

To appreciate that scene—it is in my opinion the most effective scene Greene has yet written—we should locate it in the structure of the novel. It begins a few pages beyond the mathematical middle of the book; but it constitutes the middle as well of an action which has its right beginning and its firmly established end. The basic unit in the structure of *The Power and the Glory* is the encounter: as it is in so many other novels of the generation with their picaresque tendency and their vision of man as an outlaw wandering or hastening through an anarchic and hostile world. In *The Power and the Glory,* as in *Bread and Wine,* the plot is episodic and consists of a succession of encounters between the harried protagonist and a number of unrelated persons—while within that disorderly succession, we observe a pattern of three dominant and crucially meaningful encounters.

We first see the priest when, in disguise, he sips brandy in the office of Mr. Tench, the morose expatriate dentist. We follow him, episode by episode, as he is hidden and given food by Coral, the precocious daughter of an agent for a banana company, Captain Fellowes, and his miserable death-haunted wife; as he arrives in the village which is the home of the woman, Maria, by whom he has had the child Brigida; as he travels onward in the company of a "mestizo," the yellow-toothed ignoble Judas who will betray him to the police; as he is arrested and released and fights his way over the mountains to freedom in a neighboring state and the comfortable home of Mr. Lehr and his sister, German-Americans from Pittsburgh, in charge of a mining operation; as he is enticed back across the border of Tabasco to attend the death of James Calver, an American murderer who has been fatally wounded by the police; is arrested again by a Lieutenant of the police, taken back to the capital city and executed. Tench, Coral, Maria, the Lehrs, Calver: these are all strangers to each other. The episodes with each of them thicken and expand the novelistic design (Coral, for instance, is the priest's good spiritual daughter, while Brigida is his evil actual daughter); but the design itself is created by the three encounters between the priest and the Lieutenant.

These occur at carefully spaced intervals, about one-third and two-thirds through the book, and then at length in the climax. The first time, the Lieutenant—whose whole energy and authority are directed exclusively to capturing this last remaining agent of the Church—sees the priest and interrogates him; but he neither recognizes nor arrests him. The second time, the priest is arrested, but he is not recognized: the charge is carrying liquor. The third time, recognition is complete and the arrest final. But those are mere indices of a carefully constructed plot; the action is something different and more telling, and we are made conscious of it from the outset when—in separate, successive views of them—paradoxical resemblances are registered about the two men. The priest disappears wearily into the interior, giving up a chance to escape in order to minister to a sick peasant-woman and feeling "like the King of a West African tribe, the slave of his people, who may not even lie down in case the winds should fail." On the next page, the Lieutenant marches by with a ragged squad of police, looking as though "he might have been chained to them unwillingly: perhaps the scar on his jaw was the relic of an escape." Later, as he walks home alone, dreaming of a new world of justice and well-being for the children of Tabasco, "there was something of a priest in his intent observant walk—a theologian going back over the errors of the past to destroy them again." The exhausted and sometimes drunken soldier of God, the chaste and fiercely dedicated priest of the godless society: each one enslaved to his mission, doomed to his role and its outcome: these are the beings, the sistole and diastole, between whom the force of the novel is generated.

Readers of Dostoevsky or better yet of the New Testament and the Book of Revelations will easily identify them. They are the "hot" and the "cold" bespoken by the angel in lines quoted twice in *The Possessed*: "These things saith the Amen. . . . I know thy works that thou art neither cold nor hot: I would thou wert cold or hot. So then because thou art lukewarm, and neither cold nor hot, I will spew thee out of my mouth" (Revelation iii, 14-16). The Lieutenant has had the chilling vision of absurdity: "He was a mystic, too, and what he had experienced was a vacancy—a complete certainty in the existence of a dying, cooling world, of human beings who had evolved from animals for no purpose at all. . . . He believed against the evidence of his senses in the cold empty ether spaces." With a devotion only to the reality of the here and now, he is a rebel against all the misery and injustice and unhappiness he associates with the rule of a greedy Church and its insistence on the unimportance of the human lot in this world. He watches the children in the street, his love for them hidden beneath his hatred of the Church and its priests: "He would eliminate from their childhood everything which had made him miserable, all that was poor, superstitious and corrupt."

The Lieutenant, in a word, is *l'homme révolté* of Albert Camus, seen—with respect—in the unorthodox religious perspective of Graham Greene. Francois Mauriac was right, in his preface to the French edition of *The Power and the Glory,* to call it an answer in narrative terms to the widespread European sense of absurdity—to that sense as somehow the one necessary prerequisite to the struggle for social justice. *The Power and the Glory* is not perhaps *the* answer; but it does contain, among other things, a potent allegory of one of the major intellectual debates of our time. Greene too, it should be said, gives fairer and more substantial play to what he regards as the opposition — embodied in the Lieutenant — than Camus gives to *his* opponent, the crudely drawn cleric Paneloux in *The Plague*. Camus contrasts Paneloux, and his helpless appeal to divine rationality, with the rational and dignified Rieux and Tarrou; while Greene joins the upright police officer in a contest with the wavering and incompetent whisky-priest. Yet the nameless priest, consecrating moistly amidst the unspeakable heat and the detonating beetles of Tabasco, sweating his way towards a sort of befuddled glory, is of course the representative of the "hot," and the Lieutenant's proper adversary.

These two are the persons of stature in the universe of the novel, and eventually they acknowledge each other. "You're a good man," the priest says in astonishment when, at the moment of his release from prison, the Lieutenant gives him five pesos. And: "You aren't a bad fellow," the Lieutenant concedes grudingly, during the long conversations after the final arrest. Most of the other characters, those whom Greene calls "the bystanders," are the lukewarm, and their artistic purpose is, by a variety of contrasts, to illuminate the nature of the hunt. A good many of the more "regular" members of the Church, in fact, both in the past and now in the pleasant safety of another state, appear as lukewarm; *The Power and the Glory* may be a religious novel, but it is decidedly not an ecclesiastical one. The priest himself had been lukewarm in the old days, going smugly on his parochial rounds and attending the meetings of the guilds. It is only in his moment of degradation, arrested not even for being the last priest with the courage to remain in Tabasco but only as a common citizen carrying contraband, that the priest reveals the "hot," the heroic side. He does so unconsciously, out of humility and a conviction of his own unworthiness and an irrepressible sense of humor. We return to the scene mentioned above; it occurs just before the second of the three central encounters.

The whole of it should be read, and slowly, from the entrance into the cell to the departure next morning and the sudden sense of companionship even with the Lieutenant. But perhaps the following extract can suggest the remarkable interplay—not, in this case, the remote opposition—of sacred and obscene love, of beauty and extreme ugliness, of comedy and deadly peril: all of which give the scene a rich multiplicity of action beyond anything Greene had previously achieved. Just as the key moment in *Bread and Wine* occurs in the darkness of a squalid hut, so here the "epiphany" takes place in the blackness and stench of a prison.

A long train of thought began, which led him to announce after a while, "They are offering a reward for me. Five hundred, six hundred pesos, I'm not sure." Then he was silent again. He couldn't urge any man to inform against him—that would be tempting him to sin—but at the same time, if there was an informer here, there was no reason why the wretched creature should be bilked of his reward. To commit so ugly a sin—it must count as murder—and to have no compensation in this world. . . . He thought: it wouldn't be fair.

"Nobody here," a voice said, "wants their blood money."

Again he was touched by an extraordinary affection. He was just one criminal among a herd of criminals . . . he had a sense of companionship which he had never experienced in the old days, when pious people came kissing his black cotton glove.

The pious woman's voice leapt hysterically out at him. "It's so stupid to tell them that. You don't know the sort of wretches who are here, father. Thieves, murderers. . . ."

"Well," an angry voice said, "why are you here?"

"I had good books in my house," she announced, with unbearable pride. He had done nothing to shake her complacency. He said, "They are everywhere. It's no different here."

"Good books?"

He giggled. "No, no. Thieves, murderers. . . . Oh, well, my child, if you had more experience, you should know there are worse things to be."

Pinkie Brown and Major Scobie, the protagonists of *Brighton Rock* and *The Heart of the Matter,* are never seen to smile, much less to laugh; the former is in a constant state of fury, the latter of apprehension. It is the laughter, almost more than anything else, which distinguishes *The Power and the Glory*: laughter based on the recognition of God's image in man, evoked by the preposterous incongruity of it and yet leading naturally to a warmth of fellow-feeling. Here again, a similarity may be noted with the comedy and the felt companionship of *Bread and Wine;* and perhaps Silone was not wrong, after all, to turn the ridiculous Sciattap of that novel into the treacherous figure of *The Seed Beneath the Snow.* In this particular comic vision, even the traitors—even the Judases—have a clownish aspect. Contemplating the mestizo (in another passage) and recognizing him as a Judas, the priest remembers a Holy Week carnival where a stuffed Judas was hanged from the belfry and pelted with bits of tin: "it seemed to him a good thing that the world's traitor should be made a figure of fun. It was too easy otherwise to idealize him as a man who fought with God—a Prometheus, a noble victim in a hopeless war" (the very archetype, in short, of Camus' rebel). But the force of the comic consciousness in *The Power and the Glory* is indicated, properly enough at the end, when the Lieutenant, having completed his mission and arranged for the priest's execution, sits down at his desk and falls asleep. "He couldn't remember afterwards anything of his dream except laughter, laughter all the time, and a long passage in which he could find no door." It is the Lieutenant, Greene suggests, who is the trapped man, the prisoner; and the laughter he hears is surely that laughter recorded by Dante on the upper slopes of Purgatory, the chorus celebrating the release of a captive human soul from punishment and its entrance into Paradise.

The priest himself hears none of that laughter and goes to his death persuaded of practical and spiritual failure: "I don't know a thing about the mercy of God," he tells the

Lieutenant, in the phrase which rounds out each of the three novels; ". . . But I do know this—that if there's ever been a single man in this state damned, then I'll be damned too. . . . I wouldn't want it any different." It never occurs to him that if he should so far honor the mestizo as to call him a Judas, he might himself appear as a version of the man Judas betrayed. The book has been hinting as much all along, in the pattern and style of the priest's adventures. The relationship is far more pressing and elaborate here than in *Brighton Rock* or *The Heart of the Matter,* where the vigor of supernature is hardly sweetened by the figure of the intermediary and reconciler. The priest, accordingly, preaches to the poor and the meek and downtrodden across the hilly countryside; is tempted in the wilderness; is betrayed, tried, and executed. Towards the end, he too is juxtaposed with a common criminal—the Yankee killer, whose name, James Calver, echoes two syllables of the Mount on which Christ was crucified, and opposite whose picture in the prison office the priest's face grins within the halo someone had inked around it for identification. There is even a kind of resurrection in the little epilogue—about which one has mixed feelings—when a new scared priest arrives in town and is greeted with reverence by the boy Juan, who prior to the martyrdom had been a disciple of the Lieutenant. That epilogue, offering presumably the first of the priest's miracles after death, insists perhaps too much. But if the priest is associated not only with Christ but with non-Christian divinities—the god-king of an African tribe, and the surrogate for the god, the bull who was slaughtered in the early Greek ritual of sacrifice and rebirth ("Then there was a single shot . . . the bull was dead")—nonetheless, the entire pattern is artistically redeemed by a full awareness of the grotesque disproportion between the model and its re-enactment. "The priest giggled: he couldn't stop himself. He said, 'I don't think martyrs are like this.' " It is the giggle which saves both the priest and the novel Greene has written about him. For it is when he laughs that we know this slovenly rogue, this unshaven *picaro*, to be also a saint; and we know that here for once—along with only one or two other novels—the paradoxes have held firm and the immense delicate balance has been kept intact.

III

The Heart of the Matter is the most traditional of Greene's novels, in both content and construction. As such, it is obviously less representative than *The Power and the Glory;* and as such, it has a special appeal for those who mean by the word "novel" the kind of work that appeared in the nineteenth century. We note again a major paradox about second-generation writers: they are developing a rather new brand of fiction—the novel as an act of inquiry or of rebellion or of expiation, rather than a direct and unprejudiced impression of life (the novel, that is, according to hostile critics, not as a novel at all); but at the same time, they turn for support not to the experimental first generation but to its predecessors in the nineteenth century.

The paradox is further strained in the case of Graham Greene and *The Heart of the Matter*. Here, for example, is the careful delineation, not altogether unworthy of Trollope, of various discordant elements in a multi-colored society, the society of the coastal city in West Africa which Greene had known on his journey in 1935 and again as a government official during the war in 1942-43, the date of the novel's action. In *The Heart of the Matter,* there is no savage eruption out of the animal holes into the glare and open world that characterized *Brighton Rock,* and none of the rhythmic peregrinations through anarchy of *The Power and the Glory*. The incidents take place very much *within* the society of the book and involve—not proscribed outlaws but—persons of significance and authority whose intimate knowledge of each other provides much of the hero's tragic dilemma. Here, too, there is a narrative pace, leisurely but never slack, reminiscent of Greene's distant nineteenth century relation, Robert Louis Stevenson. Greene may not be a master of all the elements of fiction; but that he is a master of narrative can be doubted only by those too little interested in story-telling to be capable of discrimination; *The Heart of the Matter* is very handsomely told. Here also is an array of characters in the old tradition—and including one especially, the merchant Yusef, whose fat and candid dishonesty would have pleased Dickens and even more so Wilkie Collins. Here, in short, is a traditional, almost a conventional *novel*: which is yet a novel by Graham Greene, and something the nineteenth century should scarcely have imagined. For what the action serves to expose is not the habits of a society or the nature of the human heart (no one, says Father Rank in the epilogue, knows "what goes on in a single human heart"), but, transcending all that, the absolute mystery of the individual destiny.

"Why, why did he have to make such a mess of things?" That is the hopeless and embittered question raised on the last page by Major Scobie's wife Louise: not "Why did he?" but "Why did he *have to?*" That Scobie, the late Assistant Commissioner of Police, had made an appalling mess of things cannot be denied. *The Heart of the Matter* is the progressive account of it, from the first moment when he is passed over for promotion to the rank of Commissioner, to the disappointment of his restless, vaguely artistic wife—a disappointment so great that Scobie, in his guilt, makes a dubious if not illegal transaction with the diamond-smuggler Yusef to get enough money to send her on a trip to South Africa; to the adulterous affair with the schoolgirlish widow, Helen Rolt, on which he embarks during his wife's absence; to the now rapid deterioration of his public and private life; to the agony—for a Catholic of his temperament—of receiving the sacrament in a condition of mortal sin; to the still graver sin of despair and suicide by which Scobie ends his career. The mess is so great and Scobie's talent, at every turn, for making bad matters worse is so remarkable that the novel has occasionally been dismissed as implausible. George Orwell once wrote to the effect that no one who could get into such deep trouble so quickly could ever have had the honorable career Scobie is alleged to have had in the first place. In the sane and skeptical humanism of Orwell, the contention is reasonable; but it is a point made outside the world of the book; within that world, the issue of plausibility does not arise.

As a matter of fact, the novel offers a definite though still typically mysterious answer to Louise Scobie's question. It would not have satisfied Orwell, for it is not drawn, finally, from psychology: that Greene thinks, is not where the real mystery lies. But before approaching the real mystery, it should be said that *The Heart of the Matter* does also offer clues for a purely psychological explanation of Scobie and his conduct. He has the profile of a genuine tragic hero. He is presented as a good man, rather better than most, with an inviolable habit of justice irritating to some of his colleagues. "You're a terrible fellow, Scobie," the Commissioner tells him affectionately. "Scobie the Just." He is an able man and within limits a forceful one; and he is a strong Catholic with that special religious intensity that only Greene's Catholics (not, that is, the Catholics one thought one knew) betray. And he has a fatal flaw: but it is not arrogance or any normal form of pride; Scobie calls down ruin on himself, plainly and articulately, but not through hybris. His flaw is an excess of the quality Greene calls pity—an inability to watch disappointment or suffering in others; with this portion perhaps of pride (in Greene's view), that he feels it peculiarly incumbent upon himself to relieve the pain. In *The Ministry of Fear,* the entertaining trial-run for *The Heart of the Matter,* Arthur Rowe's troubles begin when he commits a mercy-killing—or, to stick to Greene's verbal distinctions, a "pity-killing"—to end the intolerable physical suffering of his wife. Scobie kills no one, though he feels implicated in several deaths by violence; like several other heroes of second-generation fiction, it is his fortune to harm most of those he longs to help or even to save; and his troubles begin, in the novel, with his guilty attempt to alleviate the painful disappointment of his wife.

His feeling of guilt is due partly to his failure to be promoted; but it is rooted more deeply in another failure, an inability any longer to love his wife; and it goes back, more obscurely still, to the moment when the Scobies' only child had died, and to the fact that Scobie could not be present at the death. He is a man clearly given to self-accusation, and the pattern of it thickens as the story moves forward. It might well be that the suicide, a third of the way through, of Dick Pemberton—an Assistant District Commissioner at Bamba who hanged himself and whose mode of death affected Scobie enormously—may have released in Scobie a congenital self-destructive impulse. Pembertons' name, Dicky, with which he signed the suicide note, and the nickname Louise has coyly pinned on her husband—Ticky (his real name is Henry)—blur in Scobie's mind while he lies ill with fever after attending to the Pemberton affair; and from then on, the pace of his decline is accentuated. In summary, Scobie is an attractive, a moving and a very human being, whom we accompany long enough to understand during his downfall. We can ally ourselves with him in that other kind of pity which Aristotle calls one of the two emotions properly evoked by tragedy. But it is the second of those emotions—the emotion of tragic terror—which touches Greene's real answer: the emotion aroused not by our association with the human sufferer but by our magnetized response to the secret cause of the suffering: the terror of the action of God.

The title-phrase occurs after the opening of the novel's second part, when Scobie, momentarily alone in the night-time and looking up at the stars, wonders whether "If one knew . . . one would have to feel pity even for the planets? if one reached what they called the heart of the matter?" Less than ten minutes later—unknowingly, though he does suddenly feel cold and stranger—Scobie reaches the heart of the matter and gives up forever, or at least for the length of the book, the peace of his own soul. Coming in from his revery, into the rest-house at Pende where they have brought the stretcher-cases from the torpedoed ships, Scobie is asked to stand watch over two victims who lie unconscious on two beds divided by a screen. In one bed is a six-year-old child, a girl. Looking at her, Scobie thinks again of his own dead daughter; and, overcome by pity, he begins to pray. "Father . . . give her peace. Take away my peace for ever, but give her peace." We are to understand, I believe, that God does exactly that. He gives the child the peace of death and a release from suffering, and Scobie's peace is taken away for the remainder of his earthly career. This is the book's major turning-point, when pity deepens into terror. And the human agent through whom God acts is the patient on the other side of the screen, "the young woman lying unconscious on her back, still grasping the stamp-album." It is Helen Rolt, whom pity and loneliness will drive Scobie to make love to, in an affair which so torments Scobie's Catholic conscience that only an overdose of tablets can rescue him.

Here, as in *The End of the Affair* and *The Potting Shed,* God moves in a singularly Mephistophelean manner, His wonders to perform—a deity with whom one bargains away one's peace or love or beliefs, for the life of someone else. In a letter to French Christian existentialist Marcel Moré, Greene puts Scobie's case plainly enough: "Obviously one did have in mind that when he offered up his peace for the child it was genuine prayer and had the results that followed. I always believe that such prayers, though obviously a God would not fulfill them to the limit of robbing him of a peace for ever, are answered up to the point as a kind of test of a man's sincerity and to see whether in fact the offer was merely based on emotion." Literary criticism does not invite us to scruple over Greene's religious orthodoxy or lack of it; our much more limited question is simply the dramatic effectiveness of any religious opinion he happens to show. On this ground, *The Heart of the Matter* should be reckoned as successful —and precisely by implying, no doubt heretically but with a sort of gathering force, a terrible tension between the divine and the human, a sombre and disturbing modern version of the Greek tragic tension between fate and freedom. As in almost everything Greene has written except *The Power and the Glory* the supernatural power and the human religious impulse work against the purely human inclination: even when the result is an awe-inspiring fulfillment, the granting of a wish. We may be dismayed that things are seen to be happening so, but that they are seen dramatically cannot be doubted.

Greek classical tragedy customarily ended by a choral acknowledgment of the unsolvable mystery and the purgatorial terror. Father Rank performs that function in *The Heart of the Matter,* in the epilogue Greene has characteristically tacked on to ensure our befuddlement over the exact meaning of the events. "For goodness' sake, Mrs. Scobie, don't imagine that you—or I—know a thing about God's mercy. . . . The Church knows all the rules. But it doesn't know what goes on in a single human heart." Again, the institutionalized Church is opposed in the name of the religious mystery; and again, the sheer incomprehensibility of God's mercy and grace is the aspect insisted upon. Again, too, the hero, moving doggedly towards disaster, is oddly associated with the figure of Christ; in the manner of *Brighton Rock* rather than *The Power and the Glory,* for we are once more in a universe without intermediaries. The role of Judas is played out by the English government spy, Wilson, who covets Scobie's wife as well as reputation for integrity; and Scobie tries desperately to condone his act of despair by seeing in it an imitation of Christ: "Christ had not been murdered: Christ had killed himself: he had hung himself on the Cross as surely as Pemberton from the picture rail"—a notion which turns up later along with the suicide in *The Living Room.* All these items provide the reader, as planned, with a full measure of uncertainty: about Scobie's conduct in this world and his chances in the next. It is suggested in the last lines that Scobie may really have loved God; and it is suggested that God may be the only being he did love. The night before he goes to Pende and the dying child and Helen Rolt, we hear Scobie murmuring the incomplete phrase as he falls asleep, "O God, bless . . ." and later, another incomplete phrase as he falls senseless and dying: "Dear God, I love. . . ." Not even the reader, who knows more about Scobie than any one else, can be sure of the objects of those verbs.

Psychology thus yields to a dark theology, the pity to the terror, the human sufferer to the secret cause. All we are meant to know is that we know nothing; that is the answer to Louise's question. Pinkie Brown *almost* certainly is damned and he was without any doubt a vicious and wicked young man. The Mexican priest is almost certainly saved, and he was one of the most curiously sympathetic figures in modern fiction. We conclude, about Henry Scobie, in a purging sense of the unguessable nature of human conduct and divine intervention. Insofar as they do constitute a trilogy, Greene's three novels reverse the direction of the greatest religious trilogy, *The Divine Comedy*. Dante's poem moves from ignorance to knowledge, from discord to harmony, from unspeakable darkness to overwhelming light. Greene's "trilogy" moves stealthily deeper and deeper into the darkness, moves through the annihilation of our confidence in human knowledge to a helpless awareness of impenetrable mystery, moves from the deceptive light to the queerly nourishing obscurity. All the truth of things, for Greene, lies hidden in the darkness: whether of slum-ridden Nelson Place, of a squalid prison cell in Tabasco or of a West African night of wonder and despair. Scarcely less mysterious is Greene's achievement of making visible in that darkness, and exactly by means of it, the unforgettable drama of extraordinarily living human beings.

NOTES

1 This essay forms part of a chapter on Graham Greene in a forthcoming book, *The Picaresque Saint: Representative Figures in Contemporary Fiction.* The book deals in order with the work of Moravia, Camus, Silone, Faulkner, and Greene—members of what the book calls "the second generation," to distinguish it and them from the earlier generation of Joyce, Proust, Mann, and others. References in the present essay to the second generation and the writers mentioned should be understood as having more meaning in context.

About half a dozen sentences in this essay have appeared, in somewhat different form, in my discussion of earlier phases of Greene, in the *Kenyon Review,* Winter, 1957.

2 This notion will be developed in rather different terms by Robert Kelly of the University of Indiana, in a forthcoming study. I am indebted to Mr. Kelly for several stimulating conversations about Greene.

3 In *The End of the Affair,* the writer Maurice Bendrix, who on occasion speaks for Graham Greene, is asked about this: "You used the stream of consciousness in one of your books. Why did you abandon the method?" "Oh, I don't know," Bendrix replies in his supercilious way. "Why does one change a flat?" Because, one supposes, one does not belong there.

4 The film version of *Brighton Rock,* or so I am told, introduces a suggestive change in the matter of the phonograph record. The words recorded by Pinkie in the film go something like this: "You may think I love you, but to me you are just an ugly brat, and I hate you." When Rose plays the record (a moment left to our appalled imagination in the book), the needle sticks in the groove, and the voice is heard saying, "You may think I love you I love you I love you. . . ." A purely mechanical trick, but a device which does hint at the mixture of loathing and attraction which is Pinkie's real and bewildered attitude to Rose.

5 The image of enemy troops fraternizing is widespread in contemporary fiction. It recurs in *The Heart of the Matter,* is an actual event and a key experience in Malraux's *Les Noyers de l'Altenberg,* and is elaborated into book-length allegory in Faulkner's *A Fable.*

6 I am indebted to Mr. Herbert Haber, a former student, for this phrase and for working out in detail a suspicion we

both shared about the structure of *Brighton Rock*. See Mr. Haber's essay in this issue of *Modern Fiction Studies*.

7 "To think that God himself had become man. Minty could not enter a church without the thought, which sickened him, which was, more than the agony in the garden, the despair upon the cross."

Dominick P. Consolo

MUSIC AS MOTIF:

THE UNITY OF *BRIGHTON ROCK*

No intelligent reader today still considers *Brighton Rock* merely a detective story with theological shadings. What emerges clearly from the muddle of the book's publication—in America as an "entertainment" and in England as a "novel"—is that Greene wrote better than he knew, or at least better than his American publishers knew. In an article ("The 'Trilogy' of Graham Greene," *Modern Ficton Studies,* III [Autumn, 1957], 198-203) R.W.B. Lewis comes close to doing the book full justice by laying bare its ethical center and by defining the characters of Pinkie, Rose, and Ida Arnold. He does, however, slight the structure of meaning in setting up what he calls a "relation between the detective story and the tragedy." The more than implicit suggestion is that what began as an "entertainment," another story of a young killer (like that of Raven in *A Gun for Sale*) ended up as a quality novel. Indeed, he contends that as "Pinkie's perils and his ambitions enlarge, the very design of the book shifts and reforms." This, curiously, repeats the book's progress in publication from "entertainment" to "novel" and brings us round full circle. Now whether or not Greene wrote better than he knew, the book does have a unity of design: it is discovered in the repetition and recurrence of song titles and lyrics that, acting as a motif, fabricate a consistent pattern of meaning.

The motif unites the book's design in reiterating the theme made manifest in the conflict between the antag-

Reprinted by permission of *Renascence,* XV (Fall, 1962).

onists, Pinkie and Ida. As one would suspect from their essential polarity—Ida jocular and fun-loving: "It's a good life"; Pinkie bitter and splenetic: "Of course there's Hell"—their associations with and reactions to music reveal their diametrically different values. Being the element common to both characters, the music motif is woven naturally into the narrative line and becomes the means of conjoining Pinkie and Ida in consequence of the book's theme, for the purpose of contrasting their moral realms—the religious and the secular. Thus the motif functions as a stitching agent that brings the values of these two realms to bear on the immediate action and makes the conflict meaningful on a second level. By preparing for and sustaining the necessary theological allusions and echoes, the secular values which Ida Arnold upholds in terms of right and wrong can be measured against moral absolutes which nullify them in terms of good and evil. The motif is strengthened by the use of moralized landscape, battle imagery, and the author's own statements, but it is itself the prime agent for defining the book's controlling theme. As the motif makes clear, there is no shift in design; even Pinkie's perils and his ambitions cannot be said to enlarge. He wants to be rich, to be respected; and his peril is no greater as the result of two murders (Hale and Spicer) than it was for one. His real peril, consistent and unchanging, parallels the moral issue of the book: that "between the stirrup and the ground," as Pinkie is fond of quoting "he something lost, and something found." But whether that something lost—his soul—can be found and saved becomes less probable with each compromise and constitutes his *real* peril. The music motif illuminates from the beginning that what motivates Pinkie is the clash between his early religious training and the wish to assert himself in the experiential world. Not without a certain irony (since Pinkie is preternaturally unable to enjoy the world's pleasures), his reaction to music reveals the struggle within himself of the same quarreling elements that exist between him and Ida.

The informing nature of the music is evident whenever Pinkie or Ida command a scene. With Ida, one need not labor the obvious ("One night—in an alley—Lord Rothschild said to me"): the songs she sings reflect the immediate pleasures that govern her life; with Pinkie, it is another matter. An aura of mystery attends his violent reactions in general and to music in particular. Not until Part II when he confides in his teenage girl friend, Rose, about his Catholic heritage is the full significance of the music made known. Yet one can trace the implications that associate it, by quick juxtapositions of dialogue and action, with religion.

It is with the reporter Fred Hale, the betrayer of Pinkie's former leader to a rival gang, now fearing for his life and searching for the security of companionship that the motif appears. "Somewhere out of sight a woman was singing: 'When I came up from Brighton by the train': a rich Guiness voice, a voice from a public bar." In the voice, in the song are revealed much of what we learn later about "Lily"—Ida Arnold. Hale watches her with envy as she continues singing cheap and suggestive ballads, an "inexhaustible supply," when suddenly he hears another voice behind him say: " 'Fred,' . . . 'Fred.' " It is "the boy" Pinkie. Both Pinkie and Ida enter first as voices and both are preceded by lines of song. As Ida begins another song the frightened Hale notices the boy "watching the woman with an expression of furious distaste . . . as if hatred had been momentarily loosened like handcuffs to be fastened around another's wrists." Hale tries to joke: " 'A cheery soul.' 'Soul' the boy said, 'You've no cause to talk about souls.' " Hale tries to bribe Pinkie with the offer of ten guineas, the prize his paper gives daily to whoever recognizes him on his publicized rounds as the reporter "Kolley Kibber," as from the bar come the lyrics: " 'We met—'twas in a crowd—and I thought he would shun me.' 'Christ,' the boy said, 'Won't anybody stop that buer's mouth?' "

The religious associations that any kind of music has

for Pinkie are noticeable in these illustrations but only implied; to make them more specific at this point would destroy the mystery that envelops him. He still is referred to merely as "the boy." And yet, a less tenuous association must be made if his reaction to music is to be of telling importance. Ida's voice continues to drift through the bar: "'I wore my bridal robe, and I rivall'd its whiteness.' The boy rose furiously and, giving way to a little vicious spurt of hatred—at the song? at the man?—he dropped his empty glass onto the floor. 'The gentleman'll pay,' he said to the barman and swung through the door of the private lounge. It was then Hale realized that they meant to murder him. 'A wreath of orange blossoms. . . .' " "Souls" and "Christ" and "bridal robe"; the allusions are beginning to pile up. Further, consider Pinkie's savage rage and the deliberate irony levelled at Ida through the lyrics. These are hardly happenstance, as Greene's interjections make clear. Why else introduce the directive questions—"at the song? at the man?" Having given us the hint, he quickly shifts the focus to Hale, then draws on another song to arrest the action and to underscore the moment that ends the scene. These opening pages establish the nature of the motif and set the pattern for its recurrence. Since it contributes to tone, informs character and supports the action, one would be surprised indeed not to find it recurring again.

Ida, of course, continues her songs throughout the novel. Having attached himself to her for protection, Hale disappears even while the whiny voice rehearses: "One night—in an alley—Lord Rothschild said to me" from the steps leading down to the Ladies'. Minutes later in a new scene, we are given a description of Pinkie in terms alternately realistic and rhetorical. An orchestra sounds in the background and his reaction to the music is notable: "a movement in his belly; the violins wailed in his guts." It evokes religious associations. Shelves of dolls at the shooting gallery look "like Virgins in a church repository," and he thinks, "Hail Mary . . . in the hour of our death," even while setting up a phony alibi with the stall-man at the gallery for the time of Hale's murder. The religious allusions echo in our ears. And later, at Snow's restaurant where Pinkie goes to frighten the teenage waitress—Rose, who is completely innocent and good but who, inadvertently, has seen one of the mobsters pose as Hale—music gives rise to a baroque image of great power that transmutes the common setting of the restaurant into an hyberbole of the world's vulgarity. "The wireless droned a programme of dreary music, broadcast by a cinema organist—a great *vox humana* trembled across the crumby stained desert of used cloths: the world's wet mouth lamenting over life."

Ida now begins her private sleuthing and drives Rose and Pinkie together: good and evil forming an alliance against Ida's temporal standards of right and wrong. The recurrent strains of music sustain the alliance by preparing for the moment when Pinkie will confide in Rose and reveal the haunting memory of his lost childhood. He waits for her on the pier, a little way from the concert hall where a band is playing. "Only the music made him uneasy, the cat-gut vibrating in the heart"; " 'That music'; it moaned in his head in hot electric light, it was the nearest he knew to sorrow . . ."; and all the while he is fingering a bottle of vitriol in his pocket, "his nearest approach to passion," objectifying the radical disjunction within himself and between him and the world. When Rose finally arrives he propels her away from the pier, "the music drifting landwards, grief in the guts," angered by the tune of the orchestra, the suggestive lyrics: "lovely to look at, beautiful to hold, and heaven itself." Coming to the foreground in infinite variation the music speaks to him urgently now at the dance hall, his conflict between irreconcilable opposites projected through gesture: "one hand caressed the vitriol bottle in his pocket, the other touched Rose's wrist." Then in a climactic moment, all that the music summons up is revealed:

'Why I was in a choir once,' the boy confided, and suddenly he began to sing softly in his spoilt boy's voice: 'Agnus dei qui tollis peccata mundi, dona nobis pacem.' In his voice a whole lost world moved; the lighted corner below the organ, the smell of incense and laundered surplices, and the music. Music, it didn't matter what music—'Agnus dei,' 'Lovely to look at, beautiful to hold,' 'the starling on our walks,' Credo in unum Dominum'—any music moved him, speaking of things he didn't understand.

The confession is made against the dark of a thunderous storm and reveals the pathetic vestige of Pinkie's religion —a shred of song—the nostalgic remains of a reality which brooks no compromise with the world of Brighton.

As it threads through the action in a recurrent pattern, the music motif weaves the theological concept of moral absolutes deftly into the narrative. We recognize in this concept, too, the active force that prompts Pinkie's extreme behavior, adding a note of credibility to his vitriolic bitterness and tempering his sadistic portrait. Sin is a reality for him and its punishment assured. Although he is never quite certain of heaven, he is convinced "there's Hell." But always there is Ida, harassing Rose with questions; Spicer, frightened by his part in Hale's murder, asking to be let out of the gang. The mounting pressure forces Pinkie into violent action, but not before the alternate way of his religious world is evoked. The past is summed up, as if in desperation, by sounds only akin to music: the rhythmical "little creaking leathery movements" that come from Spicer's tiny room moments before Pinkie kills him by pushing him through the banister at the top of the stairs. "The words, 'Dona nobis pacem,' came to mind; for the second time he felt a faint nostalgia, as if for something he had lost or forgotten or rejected." What allegorical suggestions rise out of this scene—the tiny room (the confessional box), the common room (the last supper), the broken prayer, and Spicer spread-eagled under the broken banister—these are surplus meanings which posit the result of Pinkie's actions in terms of eternity and damnation. For in having certain knowledge of good and evil acts, in turning his back on confession and repentance, in not heeding, that is, the insistent call of the music he crucifies Christ again.

If an allegory is implicit in the unique associations which music and sounds have for Pinkie, it is not that the motif accretes new meanings as it recurs, but rather that it emphasizes the growing distance between what he really desires, yet ignores or rejects. With each new commitment to a way of life antithetical to his nature, he begins to understand the enormous consequences that attend the choice he has made. What a long way he has come from the opening situation in the bar when the anger in his guts "at the song?" first revealed his inner conflict. This, one needs to remember, was before the murder of Fred Hale, when Pinkie was still free from mortal sin. In choosing the way of violence instead of the way of "peace," he merely compounded his conflict. The novel's epigraph—"This were a fine reign: to do ill and not hear of it again."—cannot come true for him; evil breeds more evil and *is* heard from again. Thus the music (the sense of loss) becomes stronger and more insistent as with each "success" the ironic nature of his triumph comes home to him. A dramatic illustration is afforded in the episode of the blind band which Pinkie and his mobster friend Dallow meet shortly after the verdict of the inquest sustains the "accidental" manner of Spicer's death.

> The boy walked up the side of the road to meet them; the music they played was plaintive, pitying, something out of a hymn book about burdens; it was like a voice prophesying sorrow at the moment of victory. The boy met the leader and pushed him out of the way, swearing at him softly, and the whole band, hearing their leader move, shifted uneasily a foot into the roadway and stood stranded till the boy was safely by, like barques becalmed on a huge and landless Atlantic.... 'What's up with you, Pinkie?' Dallow said.

But Pinkie was reacting to the music and hadn't realized that they were blind; he is shocked by his own action. Images of exile follow, a wish he hadn't killed Hale;

a short recapitulation of his putative father Kite, whose carving by a rival mob left Pinkie the leader of the gang; an image of the sun staining the sky with agonies; and a symbolic gull—described as "half vulture and half dove" —diving through the iron nave of the pier. It is a portentous moment for Pinkie and the point of a resounding climax in the book, evoked and prepared for by the music. To be ignorant of its meaning, therefore, is either to assign an unmotivated viciousness to Pinkie's actions and relegate the passage to the inexplicable, or to charge Greene with an excess of rhetoric unsupported by the circumstances. But Pinkie like the band is blind, until the music makes him see what a long way he has traveled. He, too, is stranded. The distance "between the stirrup and the ground" has narrowed considerably and he is but one fall from damnation.

Although he has murdered two men, in the arbitrary (one is tempted to call them Augustinian) terms of the book's moral scheme, Pinkie still has a chance to redeem the time and to effect his salvation. He is still innocent of the sexual act with which he associates evil and corruption, his stern virginity being the very antithesis of Ida's promiscuity. And there, to strengthen the tenuous claims of religion, is Rose. But when he chooses to marry Rose, he does it to protect himself from Ida's relentless probing and gets her consent to a civil ceremony knowing full well that as Catholics the marriage and its consummation will be a mortal sin. Here the legal and temporal immunity which Pinkie gains on the narrative level becomes on the theological level his spiritual damnation. For in the person of Rose, Pinkie violates good itself by utilizing a possible agent for his redemption to meet the exigencies of the empirical world. Thus marriage and its consummation are of enormous importance in terms of the two levels in the book. If the meaning on the realistic level is clear, it is only through the surplus of meanings carried by the music that we are made aware of the allegorical nature of the sexual act.

To show how Greene brings the two levels together in a shattering climax we must begin at the point immediately preceding the marriage, as Pinkie and Dallow wait for Rose. The leitmotif of music which is important for its dominant role in the bedroom scene is represented in the ringing of a bell. Pinkie and Dallow discuss sex and after voicing his disgust, Pinkie says to Dallow: "When I was a kid, I swore I'd be a priest." This adds religion to their talk about sex and joins together the colliding opposites basic to the thematic structure. The conversation continues in this vein and Dallow asks Pinkie about his faith: "You're a Roman, aren't you? You believe. . . ." But Pinkie quickly interjects: "'Credo in unum Satanum.'" The time for the marriage approaches: "A peal of bells stopped their cracked chime and struck—one, two—." Rose appears looking "like one of the small gaudy statues in an ugly church; a paper crown wouldn't have looked odd on her or a painted heart; you could pray to her but you couldn't expect an answer." What is being rendered here is the significance of their impending marriage in terms of the book's moral scheme. Rose tells Pinkie of having gone to make a confession but that after ringing the bell for the priest, she left, knowing that they were "going to do a mortal sin." And Pinkie says in his bitter fashion, "It'll be no good going to confession ever again—as long as we're both alive." He has the sense now that the "murders of Hale and Spicer were trivial acts, a boy's game, and he had put away childish things. Murder had only led to this—this corruption. He was filled with awe at his own powers." Following the hasty marriage in a cold green room that looks like a clinic, Pinkie has this reflection: "He had no doubt whatever that this was mortal sin, and he was filled with a kind of gloomy hilarity and pride. He was himself now as a full-grown man for whom the angels wept."

Clear in themselves these foregoing illustrations also serve as an elaborate preparation for a symbolic rendering of a Communion of the damned. Pinkie's change from his earlier "credo in unum Dominum" to "credo in unum Satanum" trails in the wake of elaborate religious paraphernalia. What is needed now to complete the apostasy is the taking of a black communion.

In the romantic film to which Pinkie takes Rose after their marriage, Greene, playing on his own plot, underscores the crisis mounting within Pinkie. All of Pinkie's bitterness is projected onto the lovers in the film who are making their "stately progress towards the bed sheets." "The music moaned: 'I know in my heart you're divine.'" The ambiguity of the lyrics is marked. The actor sings a song

> . . . and suddenly, inexplicably, the Boy began to weep. He shut his eyes to hold in his tears, but the music went on—it was like a vision of release to an imprisoned man. He felt constriction and saw—hopelessly out of reach—a limitless freedom: no fear, no hatred, no envy. It was as if he were dead and remembering the effect of a good confession, the words of absolution; but being dead it was a memory only—he couldn't experience contrition—the ribs of his body were like steel bands which held him down to eternal unrepentance.

Pinkie breaks down for the first time under the pressure of colliding opposites—sex and religion—which are evoked by the music. What he doesn't understand, ironically, is that the catalytic agent to reconcile these antithetical forces is there beside him, Rose; yet he will damn himself in the sexual act not because the act itself is sinful, but because the nature of his intent is evil. To give Pinkie's damnation the scope and perspective it demands, Greene relies on the motif to establish an analogy between the taking of Rose and the consuming of the Host in the Catholic Mass. God is desecrated in this perverted rite and Pinkie becomes the devil's disciple.

The nature of Holy Communion requires a little preparatory explanation. The climax of the Roman Catholic Mass is the transubstantiation, the change of the substance of bread and wine into the body and blood of Christ to be taken in the Communion. The communicant must be duly confessed and shriven of his sins and fast for a certain period before taking the Host. During the ritual of transubstantiation, a bell is rung at each stage and before the consummation, it is rung three times. Now, what we have anticipated about the symbolic significance of the sexual act—that it is a black communion—will be apparent in the parallels from the following illustrations.

After the movie, having been turned away from the Cosmopolitan Hotel, Pinkie takes Rose to his shabby upstairs room, the only place left to go. Instead of letting himself into the house with his latchkey, however, Pinkie rings the old bell. Much is made of the bell, its age, its sound, to establish it realistically and by way of preparation for symbolic use. Inside the room Pinkie switches on the naked light and exposes the brass bed: "[Rose] took off her hat, her mackintosh—this was the ritual of mortal sin: this he thought, was what people damned each other for . . . the bell in the hall clanged." The ellipsis is in the text and this next quotation immediately follows: "He paid no attention. 'It's Saturday night,' he said with a bitter taste on his tongue, 'It's time for bed.'

" 'Who is it?' she said, and the bell jangled again—its unmistakable message to whoever was outside that the house was no longer empty. She came across the room to him: her face was white. 'Is it the police?' she said." What is most impressive and effective about this scene is that the symbology rises out of the realistic action which continues to advance the narrative. Both levels operate together to produce an ambiguity of possible meanings full of enriching irony. The bell has now rung twice. One final ring remains to complete the ritual.

He stood and waited for the clang. It didn't come again. 'Well,' he said, 'we can't stand here all night. We better get to bed.' He felt an appalling emptiness as if he hadn't fed for days. He tried to pretend, taking off his jacket and hanging it over a chair-back, that everything was as usual. When he turned she hadn't moved; a thin and half-grown child, she trembled between the washstand and the bed. 'Why,' he mocked her with a dry mouth, 'you're scared.' It was as if he had gone back four years and was taunting a school-fellow into some offense.

'Aren't you scared?' Rose said.

'Me?' He laughed at her unconvincingly and advanced, an embryo of sensuality—he was mocked by the memory of a gown, a back, 'I loved you that first time in Santa Monica. . . .' Shaken by a kind of rage, he took her by the shoulders. He had escaped from Paradise Piece to this; he pushed her against the bed. 'It's a mortal sin,' he said. getting what savour there was out of innocence, trying to taste God in the mouth: a brass bedball, her dumb frightened and acquiescent eyes—he blotted everything out in a sad brutal now-or-never embrace: a cry of pain and then the jangling of the bell beginning all over again. 'Christ,' he said, 'can't they let a man alone?' He opened his eyes on the grey room to see what he had done: it seemed to him more death than when Hale and Spicer had died.

The references to the fast, the dry mouth, the obvious ambiguity of meaning in his birthplace, the explicit consummation, the third jangling of the bell—these complete the sacrilegious rite of communion. Christ has been devoured. Pinkie feels an "odd sense of triumph" as though "an enormous weight" has lifted. He no longer fears death for he knows he is damned already. Later, when the bell sounds again it has a different modulation and a new significance: "The ugly bell clattered. . . . This was hell then; it wasn't anything to worry about: it was just his own familiar room." And finally, even as Communion strengthens a believer's faith, Pinkie feels "an invincible energy—he hadn't lost vitality upstairs, he'd gained it." The experience becomes his passport into Ida's world bringing with it a security and a satisfaction he has never known before, but he pays for it with a complete moral collapse.

In its function as a stitching agent that unifies the novel's design, the music motif is not exhausted with this climax but its main force has been spent. It continues to recur in Ida's songs as she sits victoriously at ease in her common element; but with Pinkie, significantly, the music no longer evokes the nostalgic memory of his early religious experience. There is irritation: "Don't that music ever stop?" he says several times in a scene with his underworld lawyer; but there is no recall, none that is except for the final irony. Having convinced Rose of suicide, Pinkie intones, "Dona nobis pacem," bitterly reasserting his belief in Hell because he had never had "his glimpse of Heaven. . . ."

Mary Evelyn Jefferson

THE HEART OF THE MATTER: THE RESPONSIBLE MAN

Who is this man?

His name is Scobie: he is the central character in Graham Greene's novel, *The Heart of the Matter*. He is a rather ordinary, insignificant man—stocky, gray-haired, about fifty years old. He is the Deputy Commissioner of Police, during the early 1940's, in Sierra Leone, an imaginary British colony on Africa's West Coast. He is a good policeman, careful and conscientious—Scobie the Just; but it is precisely this fact that makes him "a wonderful man for picking up enemies" at the Secretariat, and so his promotion to the position of Commissioner has been passed over. He has a wife, Louise, for whom his love has long since given way to greater pity. He has a mistress, Helen Rolt, whom he also pities. He feels a terrible responsibility for the happiness of both women. He has allowed himself to be blackmailed by Yusef, the Syrian, into passing contraband diamonds, and he has acquiesced, *almost* unknowingly, to the murder of his native servant, Ali. He is a Catholic. He is now planning to commit suicide.

Who is this man?

"I am the responsible man," he says of himself. And, certainly, this awareness of responsibility is a major motivation for Scobie. He is a man who can assume the risk of making promises—promises that he feels bound to keep, to which he must be faithful. He is, in this respect, Kierkegaard's "ethical man"—one who chooses himself,

---

Reprinted by permission of *The Carolina Quarterly*, IX, No. 3 (1957).

who defines his identity, in terms of responsible relationships with other persons.

By his marriage vows at the altar on his wedding day, Scobie had chosen to be himself in the relationship of husband to Louise. (It is significant that Kierkegaard's symbol of the "ethical stage" is marriage—the situation in which one quite literally says "I do" to another who can say "I do.") And in addition to his public vows, Scobie had made another promise:

> No man could guarantee love for ever, but he had sworn fourteen years ago, at Ealing, silently, during the horrible little elegant ceremony among the lace and candles, that he could at least always see to it that she was happy.

This promise has bound him as irrevocably as his marriage vows. As his love for Louise has receded to the point of disillusion, and as pity for her misery has taken its place, his awareness of responsibility for its fulfillment has increased.

It was Louise—lonely, rather unattractive, the "city intellectual" without friends in an alien society—who was most disappointed when Scobie failed to get his promotion. Moved by pity for the unhappy wife, Scobie borrowed the necessary money from Yusef so that she might go to South Africa for a few months to visit friends. He could know no inner peace as long as she was unhappy, and this is what he has always yearned for in the depths of his being.

> For he dreamed of peace by day and night. Once in sleep it had appeared to him as the great glowing shoulder of the moon heaving across his window like an iceberg, arctic and destructive in the moment before the world was struck: . . . Peace seemed to him the most beautiful word in the language: My peace I give you, my peace I leave with you: O Lamb of God, who takest away the sins of the world, grant us thy peace.

As the "ethical man," Scobie's relationship with God requires fidelity to the fulfillment of his moral obligations. He feels that he cannot accept God's peace until he has discharged the duties entailed by his responsibility to carry out the vows made at the altar at Ealing. His relationship to the Absolute—symbolized for him by the peace for which he longs—is relative to his absolute relationship to his ethical commitments.

So Scobie arranged for Louise's vacation. But peace was not to be his for long. Soon after Louise left, the war that had seemed rather remote from his unimportant colony finally came to his doorstep: on his Coast arrived a boatload of wounded and exhausted passengers from a torpedoed ship. Among them was Helen Rolt—a girl of nineteen, ugly and wasted from the forty-day ordeal in the open boat. Her husband of one month had been lost when the ship was sunk. Here was another object for Scobie's pity. And this emotion always involved his sense of responsibility—not evoked by the competent and beautiful but by the weak and helpless and unlovely; by the victims of the world's cruelty.

Responding instinctively, therefore, to the command of Helen's need, Scobie sought to help her. Rather than abandon her to loneliness and the lascivious Bagster howling outside her door, he entered into an affair with her—and soon heard himself making another promise: "I'll always be here if you need me as long as I'm alive." He had again entered into an ethical contract, defining himself in a meaningful way in terms of relationship to another person. But even as he committed himself, he felt the despair of the "ethical man" who recognizes that there is a contradiction in his promises which denies his ability to fulfil the obligations he has assumed. For Scobie knew that Louise's happiness — the happiness he was irrevocably sworn to seek to secure—would be shattered by his relationship with Helen. But he had now committed himself, by a vow which he felt to be equally as binding (a sure sign of the "ethical man"!), to maintain that relationship. The conditions of keeping each promise demanded the violation of the other; each excluded the possibility of fulfillment of the other.

So far, Scobie has been considered in the light of Kierkegaard's category of the ethical. It might be well to suggest that he also displays certain characteristics of the "aesthetic man." There seems to be some indication that his commitments were not wholly to Louise and Helen as persons in their own right. It is not the total structure of personality in these other selves that calls forth his willingness to accept responsibility, but it is their need of him that attracts him. To the degree that he sees them as objects in relation to himself rather than as subjects in their own right, his attitude is aesthetic. Scobie himself comes close sometimes to recognizing that there is a distinction to be made:

It occurred to him as it hadn't occurred to him, for years, that she loved him: poor dear, she loved him: she was someone of human stature with her own sense of responsibility, not simply the object of his care and kindness.

Louise returned from her vacation. A letter which Scobie had written to reassure Helen of his love fell into Yusef's hands, and he used it to blackmail Scobie into taking a packet of diamonds aboard a Portugese ship. Later, Scobie became suspicious that his boy, Ali, whom he had loved and trusted completely, knew of his adultery and might expose him, and, already enmeshed in Yusef's web, he accepted his offer to "arrange something"—what was arranged was Ali's murder. The downward pace accelerated.

Bound by his vows to Louise—not merely because he is a Catholic but chiefly because he is Scobie ("I am the responsible man"); equally bound by his promise to Helen, Scobie sinks deeper into despair the harder he tries to find a solution to his problem. As his suffering grows more acute, he trembles on the brink of Kierkegaard's "religious stage." The supposition of the possibility of fidelity to ethical commitments has been shattered, and salvation requires a new orientation.

Scobie is not innocent; he "knows"—as a Catholic—

the "right" solution: to abandon Helen, confess his adultery, be absolved, and receive Communion in the "state of grace." The Church's answer is the clear call of God—a vocation. But Scobie cannot sacrifice another human being—particularly a weak and helpless one—even for the sake of his own soul. In some dim way he associates Helen with his daughter, Catherine, who had died when she was nine years old. He is an Abraham called to sacrifice his own innocent and trusting child. But unlike Abraham, Scobie is not a "knight of faith." What is required is what Kierkegaard calls a "teleological suspension of the ethical," but Scobie cannot renounce his human responsibilities for the sake of God. He cannot will to stand in an absolute relationship with the Absolute and a relative relationship with the relative.

In the despair that lies between the ethical and religious "stages" Scobie pleads with God:

> O God, convince me, help me, convince me. Make me feel that I am more important than that child. . . . Make me put my own soul first. Give me trust in your mercy to the one I abandon.

But—"I am the responsible man." Scobie feels that he can no more trust his responsibilities to God than to anyone else.

In the Confessional Scobie had realized that he could not make a "good confession"—that he could not promise God to abandon Helen and avoid the further occasion of adultery. And so the next morning, unabsolved but unable any longer to put off going to Mass with Louise, he knelt at the altar rail to receive Communion—in a state of mortal sin.

> Only a miracle can save me now, Scobie told himself, watching Father Rank at the altar opening the tabernacle, but God would never work a miracle to save Himself. I am the Cross, he thought: He will never speak the word to save Himself from the Cross, but if only wood were made so that it didn't feel, if only the nails were as senseless as people believe. . . .

But with open mouth (the time had come) he made one last attempt at prayer, "O God, I offer up my damnation to you. Take it. Use it for them" and was aware of the pale papery taste of his eternal sentence on the tongue.

So now, believing himself damned anyway, Scobie is planning to commit suicide. He is convinced that as long as he lives he cannot abandon either Louise or Helen—even to the mercy of God. He considers his very existence a threat to the happiness of those he is trying to protect. And he cannot continue to punish God by the sacrilege he commits at the Communion rail. Louise and Helen can accept his death, he believes, without the particular suffering either would feel if he deserted her. The death of an insignificant, middle-aged man from some sort of illness is something to which one can become reconciled.

His decision is made. His answer to the call of God is no.

O God, I am the guilty one because I've preferred to give you pain rather than give pain to Helen or to my wife because I can't observe your suffering. I can only imagine it. But there are limits to what I can do to you—or them. I can't desert either of them while I'm alive, but I can die and remove myself from their blood-stream. They are ill with me and I can cure them. And you too, God—you are ill with me. . . . You'll be better off if you lose me once and for all. I know what I'm doing. I'm not pleading for mercy. I am going to damn myself, whatever that means. I've longed for peace and I'm never going to know peace again. But you'll be at peace when I'm out of your reach. It will be no use then sweeping the floor to find me or searching for me over the mountains. You'll be able to forget me, God, for eternity.

But at the very end, the final words: "Dear God, I love. . . ."

II

The problem of responsibility and attendant guilt with which Scobie struggles so desperately in *The Heart of the Matter* needs now to be examined.

The possibility of the assumption of moral responsibility pre-supposes an ontological assumption of responsibility. Scobie must first have "taken himself upon himself," willing to be a self which transcends itself, before he becomes subject to having to make moral choices. This assumption of selfhood requires a certain knowledge of good and evil; it implies loss of innocence and, consequently, the incurring of ontological guilt.

It is this problem with which Scobie is ultimately concerned. Driven to despair by the devastation of his trust in the possibility of fidelity to ethical commitments, he seeks to destroy the self he had willed to be—"the responsible man," who alone is capable of making such commitments. He sees in suicide (paradoxically, the supreme act of self-assertion) a solution to the problem of ontological guilt incurred as the result of responsible selfhood. By taking his life—by a radical refusal *to be*—he seeks the annihilation of self. In the final analysis, his suicide is not an attempt to solve the moral dilemma he faces; that effort is abandoned as hopeless, and what is sought is surcease of the ontological guilt that weighs upon him.

Moral responsibility is possible for Scobie only because of his prior willing to be a self. So willing, he is capable of pursuing values and of becoming involved in the contradiction which is the product of conflicting ethical commitments. This leads to moral guilt—that is, the recognition of one's inability to resolve the contradiction.

Scobie defines himself in terms of dedication to the idea of responsibility; it is in so doing that he "takes himself upon himself." But he then finds that that very dedication requires of him the assumption of conflicting moral responsibilties. This contradiction in purposes is impossible of resolution, and so Scobie is doomed to failure, the knowledge of which produces acute suffering and guilt, eventually leading to despair. And yet this failure is the result of his greatest achievement as a human being: choosing responsible selfhood.

Despair is the price one pays for setting oneself an impossible aim. It is, one is told, the unforgivable sin, but it is a sin the corrupt or evil man never practices. He always has hope. He never reaches the freezing point of knowing absolute failure. Only the man of good will carries always in his heart this capacity for damnation.

Scobie's concept of responsibility requires that he take upon himself the alleviation of pain wherever he encounters it. It is curiously bound up in the structure of his personality with the emotion of pity. Scobie is wholly unable to witness another's distress dispassionately; he feels compelled to "do something about it." The assumption of responsibility is an almost instinctive reaction whenever his pity is evoked.

He had no sense of responsibility towards the beautiful and the graceful and the intelligent. They could find their own way. It was the face for which nobody would go out of his way, the face that would never catch the covert look, the face which would soon be used to rebuffs and indifference, that demanded his allegiance.

Out of pity (lingering beyond love) for his lonely, dissatisfied wife, Scobie becomes embroiled with Yusef to provide for her vacation; out of pity (flowering briefly into desire) for the waif on his doorstep, he begins the affair with Helen; out of pity (distorting the truth) for a God too weak to protect Himself from the Cross, he takes his own life. He takes the responsibility of suffering so that others need not suffer.

And yet the reversed coin of this seemingly generous virtue reveals itself as a kind of vice. For Scobie's overwhelming sense of his individual responsibility implies distrust of the capabilities of others. It is a perversion of virtue; it is, in effect, pride in masquerade. Louise perhaps, with the proper kind of encouragement, could have mastered her disappointment and matured in the process; Scobie's misdirected pity and comforting lies denied her this opportunity for development. Helen perhaps, with the help of sincere friendship, could have withstood the advances of Bagster until her ship sailed for England and safety; Scobie's intervention taught her the ways of deceit and bitterness. And God, certainly, has survived the flagellation of mankind for an eternity.

Of course, if Scobie had acted otherwise than the way he did, he would have been a different self—and that would be another book! But two points are attempted here with the suggestion of different courses of action: first, that there existed the possibility of choice in the responses Scobie made to the situations confronting him; and second, that his misuse of his real freedom—the freedom to accept his existence and vocation as the gift of God—constituted his sin.

Scobie failed to comprehend the significance of his freedom. He saw it restricted and coerced by God rather than by the contradiction in his pursuit of the cross-purposes demanded by fidelity to his egocentric concept of himself. To be true to himself—to "the responsible man" he chose to be—he had to make certain promises which, by their very nature, contradicted each other. And when faced with the failure that is the inevitable result of such contradiction, he still could go no further than to reassert his selfhood with all its entangling moral responsibilities.

> If you made me, you made this feeling of responsibility that I've always carried about like a sack of bricks . . . I can't shift my responsibility to you. If I could, I would be someone else.

What Scobie failed to see was that his moral obligations were not imposed upon him by God. But although he did not recognize that his feeling of responsibility was of his own choosing, he did realize that it was what defined the identity by which he knew himself.

It has already been suggested that Scobie's excessive sense of responsibility indicates distrust of the resources of others. It is a presumption of superior strength in himself in contrast to the weakness he sees in others. He is the "iron man"—the man who does not really need anyone, the man who requires no props, who prefers not to have around him the accumulation of intimate, personal possessions which serve as crutches for the feebler personality. All of this is underscored by the interaction, mentioned before, between his feeling of pity and his sense of responsibility.

In addition to being unable to trust other persons, Scobie is also unwilling to trust God. And it is this which constitutes his ultimate sin. He lacks faith in God's ability to take care of those for whom he considers himself alone responsible. Rather than surrender any part of that burden to the mercy of God, he will forego salvation. As he moves toward suicide, God speaks to him through his despair:

> You say you love me, and yet you'll do this to me—rob me of you forever. I made you with love. I've wept your tears. I've saved you from more than you will ever know; I planted in you this longing for peace only so that one day I could satisfy your longing and watch your happiness. And now you push me away, you put me out of reach. There are no capital letters to separate us when we talk together. I am not Thou but simply you, when you speak to me; I am humble as any other beggar. Can't you trust me as you'd trust a faithful dog? I have been faithful to you for two thousand years. . . . One of them will suffer, but can't you trust me to see that the suffering isn't too great?

But Scobie replies:

> No. I don't trust you. I love you, but I've never trusted you.

Scobie's hybris, then—his sin—is this defiant lack of faith which seeks to limit the infinitude of God to the finite bounds of his own egocentric conception of His power. He seizes God's gift of freedom to be a self as a right belonging to him, and he perverts it to his own uses in a gesture of defiance. Brought to despair by the impasse of his ethical commitments, two courses are open to him: self-damnation by defiance or salvation by faithful repentance and acceptance of freedom as a gift. Scobie despairs—and takes the former course in the most radical way possible.

III

So Scobie's story ends with his suicidal death and, consequently, his eternal damnation. Or does it?

As a Catholic, Scobie "knows" what he is doing. He is sure that he is cutting himself off forever from the presence of God—that he is damning himself for all eternity never to know the blessed peace for which he had yearned. He expects hell to be a "permanent sense of loss." From this point of view, his story must be viewed as really tragic, because his death is seen as complete and ultimate annihilation. As he wrestled with God in the last days of his life, there was no doubt in Scobie's mind that this was what his suicide would mean.

But earlier in the story there had been an intimation that Scobie was not so sure that suicide irrevocably condemned one to suffer eternally the loss of God.

> The priests told you it was the unforgiveable sin, the final expression of an unrepentant despair, and of course one accepted the Church's teaching. But they taught also that God had sometimes broken his own laws, and was it more impossible for him to put out a hand of forgiveness into the suicidal darkness and chaos than to have woken himself in the tomb, behind the stone?

Scobie, at this point, comes close to "the heart of the matter."

The paragraph quoted above seems to point to the last pages of the book when Louise, having discovered that Scobie's death had actually resulted from suicide rather than angina, talks hopelessly with Father Rank:

> "He must have known that he was damning himself."
> "Yes, he knew that all right. He never had any trust in mercy—except for other people."

"It's no good even praying . . ."
Father Rank clapped the cover of the diary to and said, furiously,
"For goodness' sake, Mrs. Scobie, don't imagine you—or I—know a thing about God's mercy."
"The Church says . . ."
"I know the Church says. The Church knows all the rules. But it doesn't know what goes on in a single human heart."
"You think there's some hope then?" she wearily asked.
"Are you so bitter against him?"
"I haven't any bitterness left."
"And do you think God's likely to be more bitter than a woman?" he said with harsh insistence, but she winced away from the arguments of hope.

Scobie's Catholicism is a crucial element of his particular story, and it must be taken into consideration in any attempt to understand the nature of the conflict which engages him. But a broader application, not associated with a particular creed, can be made of the general theme of man's self-damnation and the possibility of his redemption.

Unlike pagan thought, which found the ultimate source of meaning—the fundamentally divine—in the prescriptive law of impersonal order, Biblical thought finds the ultimate source of meaning in the sovereign and creative will of a personal God. Because the will of God is sovereign, it cannot be said to be "known" in the sense that pagan law was thought to be known; because it is creative, it cannot be said to be static or "closed" in the sense that further possibility is ever ruled out. This is the idea suggested by Father Rank. The Church knows "the rules," but it cannot know—that is, it cannot encompass with the human understanding—the infinite possibility of the absolutely free and active will of God—which may offer mercy even for a finally repentant Scobie. To know is to limit—to draw a line between that which is known and that which is not known. If the line cannot be drawn, knowledge, as such, is not available, and only faith—which draws no lines—remains as the irrational response to the vast mysteriousness of the divine. Faith does not restrict, does not presume to know what cannot be known: it simply acknowledges that anything may be possible to the sovereignty of a purposeful, willing God.

Because there may be, then, a sequel to the final chapter of Scobie's story that has not been written; because there is yet the possibility that God might "put out a hand of forgiveness into the suicidal darkness and chaos," *The Heart of the Matter* cannot be called a true tragedy in the pagan sense. It is, rather, a serious kind of irony—as all "tragedies" may be considered from the standpoint of reference to the God of the Bible. It is ironic rather than tragic in that the eventual outcome is still in doubt. This is not to deny Scobie's torment, but to affirm that it is not necessarily the ultimate resolution. Even beyond death there is the possibility of repentance and eventual salvation by the infinite mercy of God.

Father Rank's words to Louise emphasize the irony prevailing at the very "heart of the matter," but they are not necessary to its recognition. Of greater significance is the last moment of Scobie's human existence:

> It seemed to him as though someone outside the room were seeking him, calling him, and he made a last effort to indicate that he was here. He got on his feet and heard the hammer of his heart beating out a reply. He had a message to convey, but the darkness and the storm drove it back within the case of his breast, and all the time outside the house, outside the world that drummed like hammer blows within his ear, someone wondered, seeking to get in, someone appealing for help, someone in need of him.

Karl Patten

THE STRUCTURE OF *THE POWER AND THE GLORY*

The nameless whisky priest of Graham Greene's *The Power and the Glory* is that characteristic Greene figure, *l'homme traqué,* and the novel itself has the familiar narrative line of the pursuit, but *The Power and the Glory* contains, by common consent, a wealth of dimension that is not always found in Greene's novels. It is a rich book because it is made of two distinct but interrelated structures. When I speak of structures in a context that would seem to call for the singular, my point is that *The Power and the Glory* is bi-structured, as are in fact most modern symbolic novels. As Edwin Muir has said:

> But to say that a plot is spatial does not deny a temporal movement to it, any more, indeed, than to say that a plot is temporal means that it has no setting in space. . . . The main object of the one plot is to proceed by widening strokes, and to agree that it does so is to imply space as its dimension. The main object of the other is to trace a development, and a development equally implies time. The construction of both plots will be inevitably determined by their aim. In one we shall find a loosely woven pattern, in the other, the logic of causality. [1]

More than any other novel of Greene's, *The Power and the Glory* is a book of symbolic identifications, and the spatial pattern of the novel depends entirely on this series of identifications. The priest is, obviously, at the center, and all of the other characters symbolically related to him,

---

Reprinted by permission of *Modern Fiction Studies,* III (Autumn, 1957).

as the spokes of a wheel relate to the hub. I would like to call this a "radial pattern," or, more allusively but in line with "the kingdom and the power and the glory," a "radiant pattern." And we may say further that the book "radiates" more than most of Greene's books, for there is hope and promise at the end—a strong contrast with the total loss that awaits Rose at the end of *Brighton Rock*. "Radiant," then, because that word, while it carries the original notion of the wheel, goes beyond to suggest the religious theme of the book and the central symbolic link between the life of the whisky priest and the life of Christ.

My method will be to take each of the characters who relate to the priest and to show in detail the quality and meaning of these relationships. First, though, we must see that the priest's story is remarkably like the story of Christ. He is betrayed by a Judas, whom he forgives; he enters the death-trap wittingly and willingly; he is hung, figuratively, beside a thief; and, of course, he is executed for his faith. However, the priest does not stand for Christ in any simple allegorical equation; he is Christ-like in that he has consecrated himself, as any Christ should, to live a life in the pattern of Christ. He is not the Son of God who redeems the sins of mankind, but he can redeem himself and be a witness, albeit flawed, to the Christian way in an unChristian world, an example to mankind.

Of the characters who surround the priest, I will look first at Tench, the English dentist who is stranded in the port town in which we first see the priest. He is modelled on the American dentist, Doc Winter, whom Greene describes in the *Lawless Roads*: "Without a memory and without a hope in the immense heat, he loomed during those days as big as a symbol—I am not sure of what, unless the aboriginal calamity, 'having no hope, and without God in the world.' "[2] Dr. Tench, cut off from the family he can hardly remember, is, like the priest, trapped in the dark land, the land abandoned by God. He, too, dreams of escape. In another way, he is like the priest, for "Tench was used to pain; it was his profession" (55), and amid the pain he goes on, endures. He symbolizes both a hopeless tenacity in clinging to life and the immense loneliness and desolation of the land. Ironically, it is through his eyes that we see the execution of the priest, for he is filling the teeth of the Chief of Police as the little man is dragged to the bloody wall (" 'Oh,' the jefe moaned from the chair, 'the pain, the pain' " [281]. In an unusual moment for him, Tench feels for another person and swears that he will "clear out for good," but we know that he will not; he is caught.

The lieutenant of police who successfully tracks down the priest may at first look like a perfect antithesis to the hunted man; he believes in the social revolution, he has a purely materialistic view of life, and he is fanatically anticlerical, but actually he, too, symbolizes a side of the priest's character, and fundamentally, the two men are more alike than different. Like the priest, the lieutenant has a vocation to which he has given his life. He thinks of the children of the state:

> It was for these he was fighting. He would eliminate from their childhood everything which had made him miserable, all that was poor, superstitious and corrupt. They deserved nothing less than the truth—a vacant universe and a cooling world, the right to be happy in any way that they chose. He was quite prepared to make a massacre for their sakes—first the Church and then the foreigner and then the politician—even his own chief would have to go. He wanted to begin the world again with them in a desert. (70-71)

Greene makes the likeness between the priest and the lieutenant explicit; the latters' room in a lodging house is "as comfortless as a prison or monastic cell"(25), and "There was something of a priest in his intent observant walk—a theologian going back over the errors of the past to destroy them again" (25). He is an ascetic, with a priest's horror of women. His relentless, cruel pursuit of the priest contrasts with the priest's animal-like wandering, but their roles become reversed after he has "succeeded" in catching his quarry, for he is brought to a state of confusion by the priest's quiet assurance in his faith, and on the evening of the day before the execution, "He felt without a purpose, as if life had drained out of the world" (268). However, he is a "good man," as the disguised priest tells him when the lieutenant gives him money; he has an embarrassed incipient charity, shown also in his awkward love for children. If we see how in his devotion to his calling he is like the priest, we must also see the implications of his relationship to the priest as Christ. Victor de Pange has pointed these out. He says: "*Le lieutenant n'est certainement pas au nombre des damnés. En cherchant á nier Dieu il a appris à le mieux connaïtre. Peut-être, lui aussi, est-il sur un chemin de Damas?*" (74). And we may think of this hard persecutor as the type of Saul of Tarsus, for his unsettled and purposeless state at the end of the book promises some change.

Entrapment and vocation. The third radial point is that of the priest who has renounced his vows and who knows that he is "in the grip of the unforgiveable sin, despair" (59). This is Padre José, who has submitted to the tyranny of the state and has married. Once, "he had been simply filled with an overwhelming sense of God. At the Elevation of the Host you could see his hands trembling . . . the wounds bled anew for him over every altar" (120), but now he has no function and is cut off from God. He represents, in his identifying relation to the whisky priest, the ever-present bad temptation to which the fugitive is so frequently drawn.

The whisky priest feels that he is not a martyr, but there is a martyr, albeit an ironic one, in the novel. He is the priest, Juan, whose pious life is being read aloud by a mother to her three children. Here Greene's love of irony broadens out into parody, and he has written several sanctimonious pages in the style of the adulatory biography. Although Juan is presented as a saint of the future who died for his church, his life is unreal in its inhuman charity and foresight; the authentic martyr, the whisky priest, prowls the dark streets in fear of capture and death, conscious of his weakness and his unworthiness. Greene fixes another spoke in his wheel-like structure.

The mestizo with the two yellow fangs is the Judas of *The Power and the Glory*. The priest himself recognizes him as a betrayer early in the book, and he knows, with the kind of foreknowledge that Christ had, that when the mestizo comes to bring him back from his safety across the border that he is leading him into a trap. He goes, however, not only to be present with the dying murderer, but because he knows that God does not mean him to escape, that it is his fate to remain and to die, if necessary, in Tabasco. And for the betrayer the priest has a feeling of charity. He thinks, as he helps the feverish mestizo, "Christ has died for this man, too" (126), and again, with a dry sadness, "Poor man . . . he isn't really bad enough" (238) to be a Judas; it is a shame that he damns himself for so little. But Greene's process of making identifying relations goes on, for the priest is not totally different from the mestizo, either; they are alike in that he too has betrayed. He has given up most of his sacerdotal duties and functions, he has fathered a child, and he rightly considers himself unworthy. He has betrayed certain of his solemn vows, and he is painfully conscious that he has "to go to God empty-handed, with nothing done at all" (273). This self-valuation may be false, or partly so, but it is what he genuinely feels before his death, and he has reason for feeling thus; he is well acquainted with the Judas within himself.

The children of *The Power and the Glory* also have their relationship to the priest. Brigida, the priest's young-old daughter, warped and wizened by the blighted land, and Coral Fellows, daughter of an English banana planter, both retain an odd innocence, something primal, under the fast-growing shell of their early maturity, that corresponds exactly to a hidden and harbored innocence, which is ultimately the source of his salvation, in the weary, world-racked whisky priest.

The last of the characters who radiate from the priest

is the American gunman, thief, and murderer. He is, like the priest, a criminal and a fugitive, and his photograph is hung next to the priest's on the wall of the police station: "On the wall of the office the gangster still stared stubbornly in profile towards the first communion party: somebody had inked round the priest's head to detach him from the girls' and the women's faces: the unbearable grin peeked out of a halo" (71). The priest feels that they are brothers, and it is clear that Greene has mirrored the situation of the Crucifixion (and the "first communion party" has its significance, too). While the priest tries to make the dying gunman repent his crimes, the gunman urges the priest to take his knife or his gun and fight his way out of the police trap, a passage reminiscent of Luke xxiii. 39 ("And one of the malefactors which were hanged railed on him, saying, 'If thou be Christ, save thyself and us.' ") Once again the pattern reveals itself—those around him are like the priest ("radial") and the priest is like Christ ("radiant"). *The Power and the Glory* finds its deepest source in the Incarnation.

In addition to the wheel-like structure of "radiance" there is the second structure, based on the "logic of causality." This is temporal, rather than spatial, and is based on the pursuit of the priest by the lieutenant of police and by God. It is a narrowing, narrative structure that is reminiscent of the film device of "parallel montage," [3] and it gives the novel its intensity and suspense.

This double pursuit exists on the natural level in the hunt of the lieutenant, who wishes to exterminate the last tiny residue of Catholic superstition in Tabasco, and on the supernatural level by God himself, who harries the sinful priest down the labyrinthine ways to his own salvation. Obviously, the pursuit by God cannot be pictured; we must infer this from the priest's own thoughts and from his reactions to events, which, however, he himself does not always understand, for his tenacity and his willingness to go back over the border are themselves God-given. But the natural pursuit is like that of any of

Greene's thrillers. We first see the mysterious figure of the priest at the sea-port, but not until the end of the first chapter do we understand that this obviously disguised person is a fugitive. He says, "Let me be caught soon. . . . Let me be caught," and Greene adds, "He had tried to escape, but he was like the King of a West African tribe, the slave of his people, who may not even lie down in case the winds should fail" (18).

Then, in the next chapter, Greene shifts to the pursuer, the vaguely troubled yet seemingly inflexible lieutenant, who learns of the single remaining priest for the first time. The long pursuit begins, and with it the crosscut temporal structure of the book. Over and over again we see the priest ineptly trying to perform his duties, or hiding from the police, or, finally, achieving safety by escaping across the mountains into Chiapas, the neighboring state. And over and over again we see the lieutenant plotting his campaign, taking hostages, always in single-minded pursuit. Several times their paths cross, but never does the lieutenant recognize the priest, and the priest is never apprehended; for in this book the natural pursuit is to fail, and it is the supernatural pursuit, God's hounding of the priest, that is to succeed, for the priest voluntarily chooses capture and death after he is safe; his years in the jungle have made him as cunning as an animal, and he could have escaped the law of the land, but he could not escape the law of his God.

Thus, the method of parallel montage, with its base in Greene's dark, dualistic imagination, provides a narrative structure of high intensity, the rapid line of a flight, or more exactly a fugue—for we can think of this method as contrapuntal in its weaving motion—that reaches its climax when the priest turns his mule back toward Tabasco and is finally caught in the lieutenant's trap, this fugue followed in the closing pages of the book by a large, deep *largo*.

Two structures, then: one, which flows chronologically from the beginning of the book to the end, the other, which must be pictured or diagrammed ideally. But it would be a mistake not to realize that the two constitute a fusion: temporal, drama or melodrama; spatial, symbol. There is nothing unique in Greene's combination; it is the aesthetic method of the modern novel, of all novelists of high style as Ortega would say. *Moby-Dick* is also a symbolic pursuit novel, as are many of Faulkner's novels (*Light in August, The Wild Palms,* or *The Old Man*), and the novels of such different writers as Dostoyevsky and Henry James, though perhaps not pursuit novels, make the same magic combination of space and time. There are, of course, other symbolic novels which render as little as possible to time, like Virginia Woolf's *The Waves,* which seems to exist in the vacuum of a glass bell, and which we read claustrally, relating one sensitively developed event to another, but a novel like *The Waves* is misguided in intention, for time lends life to fiction.

Aristotle first noted the necessity for an action, a temporal happening, that was significant and probable (that is, conceived and executed with a certain verisimilitude), and which made the play dynamic. Modern poetry, however, has not had as its first interest the description of an action. In content, it has been more interested in states of mind, either of the poet or of his *personae,* and in form it has developed an aesthetic that holds that all of the parts are to be related to the whole. Consequently, it has become a poetry that is allusive and infra-refracting, a poetry that renders and does not state (and modern poets discovered that the best poets of earlier ages wrote similarly), a poetry that does not immediately organize itself on the page, but rather leaves the process of organization, which is essential for comprehension, up to the reader, who must relate for himself, reread, and study.

It is this kind of poetry that the modern novel has taken over for its spatial structure, but it has combined the method of modern poetry with the Aristotelian demand for a significant action. In this combination, however, there may be an important change in one of Aristotle's criteria, for, in the interest of the spatial structure, the symbolic novelist is often willing to relinquish some of the verisimilitude than an earlier novelist would have felt essential. Faulkner and Dostoyevsky do not hesitate to describe events and characters which are, to say the least, out of the ordinary—Benjy and Prince Myshkin are sufficient examples, and they have been created to make the spatial and symbolic structures of *The Sound and the Fury* and *The Idiot* rather than to contribute primarily to the temporal and probable structures. Mental defectives and epileptics *do* exist, but Aristotle (and Fielding, Jane Austen, or Galsworthy) would not have found them appropriate vehicles for a play or a novel—and not, basically, for reasons of decorum.

Joseph Frank, who first clarified the concept of spatial structure, has pointed out the semblance of the art of primitive peoples to the art of our own century and the likeness of both to periods that "are dominated by a religion that completely rejects the natural world as a realm of evil and imperfection." Now, nothing is clearer than that Greene so regards the world and that original sin is at the very core of his Catholic and personal metaphysics. Frank adds that:

> In both cases— the primitive and the transcendental—the will-to-art . . . diverges from naturalism to create esthetic forms that will satisfy the spiritual needs of their creators; and in both cases these forms are characterized by an emphasis on linear-geometrical patterns, on an elimination of objective, three-dimensional shapes and objective, three-dimensional space, on the dominance of the plane in all types of plastic art.[4]

And he goes on to show, brilliantly and convincingly, how this generalization is applicable to literature.

Greene's whisky priest, in his namelessness, his frailty, his unsureness of purpose, his backsliding, his desire to be free from his terrible responsibility, his cowardice, and his ultimate underlying strength, is clearly of the type of Everyman, that primitive product of the late medieval imagination. And, more precisely, just as Everyman discovers on his road to the grave that he can take nothing but Good Deeds with him, so the priest must discard all but his essential faith in God. [5] Greene figures this for us by making him, in the course of the novel, literally give up or lose his various holy objects and habits; feast days and fast days, his breviary, the altar stone, a chalice, the papers that sealed him in the priesthood. All go, until he is stripped naked before his fate, a being deprived and alone —except for his God.

Greene has praised *Everyman*, and he has said of Shakespeare:

It must be remembered that we are still within the period of the Morality: they were being acted yet in the country districts: they had been absorbed by Shakespeare, just as much as he absorbed the plays of Marlowe, and the abstraction—the spirit of Revenge (Hamlet), of Jealousy (Othello), of Ambition (Macbeth), of Ingratitude (Lear), of Passion (Anthony and Cleopatra)—still rules of the play. And rightly. Here is the watershed between the morality and the play of character: the tension between the two is perfectly kept: there is dialectical perfection. [6]

And what is the difference between the morality and the play of character but the difference between a spatial and a temporal structure? The modern novel exists on the thin ridge of that watershed.

Greene has given us in *The Power and the Glory* a study of the character of the whisky priest which is itself temporal, but beyond this he has created a static, symbolic structure which is akin to allegory without ever resolving into a simple series of one-to-one equations between characters and concepts. It is this nearly allegorical structure that makes the wheel-like pattern which can best be conveyed by a diagram ("linear-geometrical patterns"), the radial, radiant, radiating pattern that forces a subtle lack of three-dimensional verisimilitude on the novel.

There is a drive in Greene's imagination here, a drive which makes him create a single priest out of the tiny shards of at least three real priests (as we know from *The Lawless Roads*) [7] and to make his whisky priest a tenacious man of God in a way that goes far beyond the stories of any of the three priests—like Benjy or Myshkin, the priest is beyond what we know or what we expect. And, in addition, Greene has, by suggestion, made an analogy, without insisting on a simple correspondence, between his priest and Christ, as Faulkner and Dostoyevsky have done with their characters.

Why is the priest nameless? And why is his persecutor, the lieutenant, nameless too? Clearly, it is because names individuate and by their very particularity assign small, local associations, while anonymity is suggestive of something larger, and, in this novel, Greene wants to be free of such limiting factors, so that, although he gives both priest and persecutor believable backgrounds, they both have typical backgrounds for what they are. In other novels Greene is apt to make use of signifying names (Anthony Farrant, Conrad Drover, Raven, Harry Lime, Rose), but here his passion inclines him more strongly than ever toward symbolization, so that if the priest is an Everyman who is to be related, by suggestion, to Christ, then the lieutenant is to be understood as a Saul of Tarsus.

Further, we see that the people whom the priest meets are all symbolic of some aspect of the human condition: a trapped man (Dr. Tench), a criminal (the American gunman), purposefulness without purpose (the lieutenant), children who cannot be well understood (Brigida and Coral), a lapsed priest (Padre José), Judas (the mestizo), a beggar with inside information (nameless, but like the priest), a pious woman (likewise nameless, but part of his old self), lovers (his temptation)—in short, like Christian in *The Pilgrim's Progress* he travels an unknown way, continually meeting portions of his own character, God-ordained obstructions or revelations which eventually help him to his death and salvation.

Although the pursuit is always present, we realize, through the priest's meetings and confrontations with these characters (who, because of the way in which Greene has presented them, would be "flat" in E. M. Forster's terms), that in back, as it were, of the pursuit there is elaborated another, deeper meaning—the structure of the radiant wheel and we would not see this if these characters were presented with full verisimilitude.

Paradoxically, however, as we read this novel we feel its roundness, especially as it is rendered in one great scene, and we recognize the all-integrating wholeness of the wheel on which Greene has based his symbolic structure.

In this scene, the priest, disguised, has been jailed, and he is thrust into a crammed, stench-filled cell. In the course of the night he hears (for he cannot see anything) aggressive, importunate people, an old man out of his mind, two people making love, a pious woman, talk of bastard children (especially painful to him), and all the voices of the world—for the cell is the world. He tells his fellow prisoners that he is a priest, and despite the fact that there is a price on his head, no one reveals him to the police at dawn. The prisoners are sullen, perhaps unhappy, about their loyalty, but we feel that there is a final goodness in their refusal to betray him which is connected with the final greatness (in the terms of Greene's own belief), and that this is related to the final generosity of God in accepting sinners into his kingdom (as we feel that the priest is accepted at the end of the book), but we could not have had this feeling if we had not been prepared for it by the evolving, poetic structure of the whole novel.

Greene has given us, in *The Power and Glory,* a fusion of the temporal and the spatial, the long, melodramatic pursuit and the slowly-developed, carefully-related radiant wheel that stands in back of the pursuit, and he has endowed this fusion with the significance that we demand of the modern novel. When we have become fully aware of the wheel and its implication, we have a knowledge of "the thick rotundity of the world."

NOTES

1 Edwin Muir, *The Structure of the Novel* (London: The Hogarth Press, 1928), p. 64. Muir uses "plot" as a synonym for "structure."

2 Greene, *The Lawless Roads* (London: Eyre and Spottiswoode, 1950), p. 156. "The aboriginal calamity" is quoted from the epigraph to *The Lawless Roads,* which is from Newman's *apologia pro Vita Sua* (New York: Modern Library, 1950), pp. 240-241. The final quotation is from Ephesians ii. 12. Greene's Mexican travel book provides us with nearly all of the raw material of *The Power and the Glory.*

3 "Parallel montage" is, according to Eisenstein, "the image of an intricate race between two parallel lines" ("Film Form" in *Essays in Film Theory,* ed. Jay Leyda [London: Dennis Dobson, 1951], p. 234). Thus, when two events are happening simultaneously, the director, in order to create the illusion of simultaneity and to heighten intensity and suspense, will crosscut back and forth from one to the other.

4 Joseph Frank, "Spatial Form in Modern Literature," in *Criticism: The Foundations of Modern Literary Judgment,* ed. Mark Schorer, Josephine Miles, and Gordon McKenzie, (New York: Harcourt Brace, 1948), p. 390 (both citations).

5 *Everyman,* in its complete emphasis on merit and its striking disregard of faith, is a pre-Reformation work. Greene's attenuated Catholicism (Jansenism? — a favorite charge) bases the issue totally on faith. It is the unwavering essential fidelity of the priest that will save him; his sinful acts and his failure to function adequately as a priest ultimately count for nothing to Greene.

6 Greene, *British Dramatists,* in *Impressions of English Literature,* ed. W. J. Turner (London: William Collins Sons & Co., 1944), p. 114.

7 For information on the three priests, see *The Lawless Roads,* pp. 11-12, 129, and 150.

Neville Braybrooke

GRAHAM GREENE AND THE DOUBLE MAN

AN APPROACH TO *THE END OF THE AFFAIR*

In Graham Greene's work no sharp divisions can be drawn between his novels, "entertainments," travel books and miscellaneous sketches and essays. They are all part of a piece, and throughout them all, in some form or other, runs the theme of pursuit. In his first novel, *The Man Within* (1929), the predicament is stated in clear-cut language: "A sense of overwhelming desolation passed over him, a wonder whether he would ever know peace from pursuit. . . ." Andrews has betrayed his fellow-smugglers to the Excise Men; he shelters in a girl's house, and she persuades him to turn King's Evidence; he does so—partly because he is in love with her and partly because he wishes to assert his own authority. For his loyalties are divided. His life has been a series of alternations between his higher and lower natures, between the spirit and the flesh. In the words of Sir Thomas Browne: "There's another man within me that's angry with me"; and it is with this duality in man's nature that Greene has always been concerned.

For instance, this duality will be found reflected in nearly all the authors from whom Greene takes the epigraphs for his books—not only in Sir Thomas Browne, but also in his choice of texts from Dryden, Auden or Edwin Muir; Cardinal Newman or Kingslake; Léon Bloy or Charles Péguy. Certainly, if the Greene epigraphs were to be collected and printed separately, a most odd, if illuminating midget anthology would result. Yet a careful scrutiny

---

Reprinted by permission of *The Dublin Review*, CCXXVI (First Quarter, 1952).

of the authors represented would reveal a common factor. Not all of them might be poets in the strict sense of the term, but in all their prose it would be possible to discern the poetic essential of intuition. More: it would be discovered that they frequently employ juxtapositions and paradoxes so as to be able to play tricks with time-sequences; to impose supernatural happenings upon natural ones; to present at one and the same instant "the real world of/ Theology and horses."[1] That last phrase is an Auden one, and there is, perhaps, a singular aptness about using it here, because there is a poetic and telegraphic concision about it which Greene has struggled to achieve in his own prose. After all it was as a poet that Greene originally broke into print.

Five years before Auden's first book of poems appeared, Blackwell's published Greene's one and only book of verse, *Babbling April.* However, by 1929 he had turned his attention solely to fiction. At the beginning of *Rumour at Nightfall,* which he brought out in 1931 three years after the appearance of his first novel, *The Man Within,* there is a passage from Traherne which provides a clue not only to this book, but to all Greene's novels—including his latest, *The End of the Affair* (1951).[2] For the Traherne extract provides, in miniature, as concise a synopsis as one can have of Greene's 1929 view of reality—a view to which all his subsequent writings have gradually lent greater strength. Here is the verse in question:

> O ye that stand upon the brink,
> Whom I so near me through the chink
> With wonder see: What faces there,
> Whose feet, whose bodies, do ye wear?
>   I my companions see
>   In you, another me.
> They seemed others, but are we;
> Our second selves those shadows be.

In retrospect, it is not hard to see how Greene has enlarged upon this conception of reality, this idea of the double man: for the hints of the double man in such early

Greene characters as Andrews, Raven, Pinkie and Arthur Rowe become fully pronounced in the whisky-priest in *The Power and the Glory* (1940), in Scobie in *The Heart of the Matter* (1948), and in Bendrix in *The End of the Affair.*

Yet in the two books following fast on the heels of *The Man Within, The Name of Action* (1930) and *Rumour at Nightfall*—both of which the author suppressed later—there is no advance: rather, so far as the expansion of the thought behind them is concerned, there is regress. Indeed, risking a generalization, these three novels might be most suitably catalogued as "European Westerns." Constantly in them men—rather poetically—look down ravines, seeing "creams of foam" gathering beneath water-falls, whilst a romantic—and somewhat poetic—atmosphere is often introduced by playing up "the love interest" in a way which has its visual equivalent in the love scenes of the pioneer silent films: "He came close to her and put his hands upon her arms and pulled her close to him." Again a good many of Greene's early similes are either forced or clichès. Here is an example of a cliché: "Outside the door patches of fleeting blue sky waved in the rain and desolation like a tattered banner"; and here is an example of a forced simile: "He tried with heavy steps to climb to her mood of laughter, but found the ledge insecure, the foothold treacherous, the fall too terrifying." At this stage there was none of that economy of language which has made some of Greene's finest writing seem as if it were as precisely worded as a telegram.

In *The End of the Affair* can be seen the fruits of the strict paring away of unnecessary words, for every adjective used in the book makes more exact the meaning intended: there are no verbal ambiguities, no loose strings. [3] Further the background of either a tropical or an asphalt jungle has been abandoned, and in its place has been substituted a "respectable" area of suburbia—Clapham Common. For the most part the action is localized, though there are excursions to Golders Green Crematorium, the

British Museum Reading Room, Rule's Restaurant and a few other "respectable" places. At any rate there is no admittance of (or to) a London underworld. On the surface as well the three central characters are eminently "respectable." There is Henry Miles, a middle-aged senior Civil Servant, and Sarah his wife (though married ten years, they have no children): there is, too, Maurice Bendrix, a mutual friend and author; and if I summarize their story it is because, adequate as the summaries have been by other critics, certain factors which are crucial to a full understanding of the novel's implications have, I would submit, been missed. The fault has lain with too close an identification of Bendrix with Greene—though let me add hastily that most critics have warned their readers to be on guard exactly against such a linking.

This is Greene's only novel up to 1951 written in the first person. Bendrix who is its narrator is a fairly successful author; but he is second-rate. That does not mean that he is not a conscientious writer nor that he does not expend as much energy and care upon his work as a good writer, because he does: in fact often second-rate writers, because they have less talent, have to apply themselves far harder to their work. On the contrary, what I wish to suggest is that Bendrix himself is somewhat second-rate and that precisely that second-rate attraction which he has for the superficial colors his whole account of his relationship with Sarah and her husband; the account is always slightly off balance. Greene is writing at one remove.

Bendrix decides to open his narrative with a picture of Henry Miles "slanting across the wide river of rain" sweltering down upon Clapham Common on a black, wet January night of 1946. But wait a second. Does Bendrix choose this moment, or does this moment choose Bendrix? For in the first paragraph of his narrative one is aware that one has entered the terrain of the double man: writing with a knowledge of past events which a reader cannot have, Bendrix from the start is capable of seeing himself as both the pursuer and the pursued; of seeing himself as both the subject and object of his experiences. Why this is so from the start becomes immediately clear if one turns to the book's epigraph. "Man has places in his heart," declared Léon Bloy,[4] "which do not yet exist, and into them enters suffering in order that they may have existence"; and in *The End of the Affair*, with its juxtapositions of time-sequences, when Bendrix chooses to begin his story those places in the heart of which Bloy speaks have come into existence for him. For in one sense when Bendrix picked up his pen the affair was over; in another, just beginning.

Unknown to Henry, Bendrix has been Sarah's lover. Then suddenly their affair ends. Henry, unsuspecting that Bendrix has ever been his wife's lover, suggests that her affections have strayed elsewhere; he has toyed—though not too seriously—with the idea of using a private detective to track down the third man. Whereupon Bendrix takes up the cue: he decides to exploit Henry's naïveté to satisfy his own curiosity—and hatred. For jealous at being dropped for another, Bendrix believes that if a third man can be found he can turn his venom outwards on Henry. A private detective called Parkis is engaged—and the pursuit is on: it also becomes a pursuit down the labyrinthine ways of Bendrix's mind. Various enquiries are made: one possible suspect is Richard Smythe, a West London rationalist preacher; another Dunstan, the head of Henry's department at the Ministry. Then the real evidence is found: it is contained in Sarah's private journal.

Book III comprises the journal. Sarah is not seen through Bendrix's eyes any longer for by this device the reader is shown her objectively. Up to now he has seen her subjectively through Bendrix's eyes, and now he can have the picture completed. It emerges that she is a woman both repelled and attracted by God, since it turns out that it was God who was the lover whom neither Bendrix, Henry nor Parkis could track down. Yet though she desires to love God more than anything else in the world, she also desires Maurice: "I want Maurice: I want ordinary corrupt human love." The journal closes on the note: "Dear God, You know I want to want Your pain, but I don't want it now. Take it away for a while and give it me another time"—a note which is but a variation on St. Augustine's great human cry: "O God, give me continence, but not yet." [5]

Purposely I should like to stop half way through this summary because having mentioned St. Augustine it reminds me that some debate has already arisen over whether Sarah is intended to be a saint. Recall: the same debate arose over Scobie—another double man, although with the other double man in Greene's fiction, the whisky-priest, the debate could not arise because his death was that of a martyr. Yet with Sarah those who argue for her sainthood have a stronger case than with Scobie because she is definitely connected with what seem miracles to Bendrix, loath as he is to admit them; and I mention the word myself with a certain caution. To take the first of these "miracles." . . .

During an air-raid Bendrix leaves Sarah in his room to slip down and see if his landlady is in the basement. Half way down the stairs, a flying bomb explodes: for a few minutes, pinioned beneath a door, Maurice lies unconscious. Then he picks himself up and returns to Sarah; the door is ajar and he stares at her crouched on the floor: "What are you doing on the floor?" . . . "Praying" . . . "Who to?" . . . "To anything that might exist." He ticks her off sarcastically: "It would have been more practical to come downstairs." But apparently she did—although, pinioned beneath the door, she felt positive that his body was lifeless: "I knew for certain that you were dead" . . . "In which case there wasn't much to pray for then, was there? Except"—as Bendrix goes on to tease her: "Except a miracle." She simply answers: "When you are hopeless enough you can pray for miracles. They happen, don't they, to the poor, and I was poor." This is Bendrix's verbatim account. Here, in contrast, is Sarah's —taken from her journal:

He hadn't been gone two minutes when there was an explosion in the street. . . . I didn't see Maurice at first, and then I saw his arm coming out from under the door. I touched his hand: I could have sworn it was a dead hand. When two people have loved each other, they can't disguise a lack of tenderness in a kiss, and wouldn't I have recognized life if there was any of it left in touching his hand. I knew that if I took his hand and pulled it towards me, it would come away, all by itself from under the door. Now, of course, I know that this was hysteria. I was cheated. He wasn't dead.

Yet when she returned to his room, she knelt down. She prayed: "Dear God . . . make me believe. I can't believe. Make me. . . . I'm a bitch and a fake and I hate myself. I can't do anything of myself. *Make* me believe." [6] Then, a moment later, she continues: "Let him be alive, and I *will* believe. Give him a chance. Let him have his happiness. Do this and I'll believe." So far Maurice has not stirred. She says, another moment later, very slowly: "I'll give him up for ever, only let him be alive with a chance"; and, as Maurice walks in, she thinks: "Now the agony of being without him starts," and she wishes that he was safely back dead under the door.

Miracle or hysteria—that is the question. Sarah's journal has a hint that it was possibly the latter, for looking back on the incident she states: "Now, of course, I know that this was hysteria." The word "hysteria" is hers, whilst that of "miracle" is first suggested by Bendrix—which is an odd juxtaposition of their attitudes, as the second half of the book shows. Anyhow, at this period, for both of them the incident of the flying bomb remains a tantalizing open question. Greene continues to write at one remove.

So much for the first miracle, though, as I say, I use the word with some misgiving; for it is Bendrix who has first suggested it. Now, to return to my summary. . . .

Sarah dies of a cold, and shortly afterwards Henry asks Bendrix to share his house with him: in the meantime he wants Bendrix to help him with the funeral arrangements. "It's been an awful day, Bendrix. You know, I've never had death to deal with. I always assumed I'd die first—and Sarah would have known what to do. If she'd stayed with me that long. In a way it's a woman's job—like having a baby." So, with the helplessness which affects men on these occasions, they plan the funeral arrangements together. Smythe, the rationalist preacher, calls and asks to see Sarah. Grudgingly, Bendrix consents; but before he goes to see her laid-out in the room above, he begs Bendrix to do something for her. "Let her have her Catholic funeral. She would have liked that." Besides, "It always pays to be generous [to the dead]." For, according to Smythe, just before she died she had gone to see about being "instructed." A few minutes later when Smythe returns to the room, Bendrix notices that his right hand is clenched: it contains a lock of Sarah's hair . . . and Bendrix now sees her as a body, "a piece of refuse waiting to be cleared away: if you needed a bit of her hair you could take it, or trim her nails if nail trimmings had value to you. Like a saint's her bones could be divided up—if anybody required them. She was going to be burnt soon, so why shouldn't everybody have what he wanted first?"

But the outburst subsides for the time being; on returning to his room on the other side of the Common he finds a letter from Sarah. She had written it to him before she died, but had mis-addressed it—and hence the postal delay. In it she tells Maurice that she has been to see a priest to consider being "instructed" and to see if she could have an annulment. His replies come to her like *cul-de-sacs* where she had thought lay avenues of hope. Her Registry Office marriage with Henry *does* count. "No, no, no," the priest said, "I couldn't marry you, not if I was going to be a Catholic."

So one half of Bendrix is satisfied; physically the affair is over and from a material point of view all is ended as a love story; it is the ideal point for the professional writer to close his tale.

However, "there's another man within me that's angry with me"; there are those inner voices which aggravate the outer conflicts—"our second selves" of which Traherne spoke. Bendrix knows that it would be false to bring down the curtain here; he is a pessimist, with an awareness, if not an acceptance, of the knowledge that Hell lay about him in his infancy; his vision of the world is of a battle-field—not a rose-and-water utopia where peace reigns. As one can have a "phoney" war (and Bendrix had lived through part of one as a civilian), one can have a "phoney" peace—inside and out; and to have cut short his tale at this point would have only given Bendrix a "phoney" peace of mind. It would have meant too a "phoney" account of the affair. For he is like a man being pursued; he cannot turn back, but must go on. [7] Once he had picked up his pen, all other courses became denied to him: an irrevocable decision had been made.

Artistically, what follows could conceivably be called an epilogue—though I myself believe that to accept the remaining chapters in this light is to miss the main purpose of the book. They conclude nothing: and if they answer some questions, then it is only to ask more. The affair is not over nor has Bendrix's love gone sourly dead. His love which at the end—though against his will—has been a forced chaste love is beginning to bear fruit; it has not been without rhyme or reason. Now of this effect Bendrix is quite aware and in his heart of hearts is prepared to admit it; but resentment and bitterness are still there. Suffering may have brought new places into existence in his heart, but his passions have not been fully cleansed: he remains a double man, and concupiscence is always daggering him. For when Bendrix originally became interested in Sarah it was because he wanted to study a senior Civil Servant first-hand for a short story and he had thought the easiest way to "get the copy" was through such a man's wife. This admitted and the affair having worked itself out as it did, Bendrix finds it disturbing to discover that it has repercussions.

Those repercussions are the cure of a patch on Smythe's cheek by the application of Sarah's lock of hair and the cure of Parkis's son by what to the boy—if he was grown and educated up enough to know the phrase—could only be described as the divine intervention of Mrs. Miles. (The private detective and his boy had always had much more than a mere sneaking regard for her.) These are spectacular cures and, although publicly Bendrix is not prepared to admit that they are miracles—he fobs off enquirers with half-truths about them—, it is also quite apparent that he really does more than half believe that they are miracles. His talk to Henry about coincidences such as seeing "two cars with the same figures side by side in a traffic block" despite "ten thousand possible numbers and God knows how many combinations," is pure bluff.

That Greene has been able thus to present the double man in Bendrix is some indication of his versatility as a craftsman; but behind this achievement there lies yet a greater. The two miracles in the second half of the book of which the most are made are exactly two which contain that superficial element which would appeal to the second-rate in Bendrix; and, for sure, as he himself a quarter thinks, the cures may have been largely a case of cured hysteria. [8] Remember that Greene is not to be identified with Bendrix for this is fiction reported at one remove and, remembering this, look behind Bendrix's narrative, see it at two removes, and it will be noticed how cunningly the double man has been brought out in Bendrix. For within Bendrix's narrative there are two kinds of miracle which pass by almost without comment. One of them occurs at Golders Green Crematorium when Bendrix, having met a young girl in corduroy slacks, decides that he will seduce her that night (concupiscence is still daggering him): then subsequently after the service he thinks better of it; prays to Sarah for help. Suddenly Sarah's mother turns up; she has come to London for the cremation and Bendrix excuses himself to Sylvia on the ground that he must dine with Mrs. Bertram; an alibi has been provided.

At the time the incident makes little mark upon Bendrix—although he does refer to it once in passing in the last chapter; but it never, like the cured cheek, takes a foremost place in his memory. The other kind of miracle receives no comment whatever. It occurs in Sarah's journal.

In it she relates how on the day that she decides to go off with Maurice—having written a farewell letter to her husband—fate or coincidence brings Henry in half an hour earlier than usual; he has a dreadful headache and just as Smythe's patch on his cheek awoke Sarah's pity, so Henry's premature return prevents her from being cruel enough to give him the letter directly; and because she cannot give him the letter directly, the delay makes the moment of giving it impossible. Her pity awakened to its fullest, she sees poor Henry as "one of misery's graduates"—to use a term coined previously by Bendrix.

In the case of Mrs. Bertram's appearance at the cremation service and Henry's headache, I have used the words "alibi", "fate" and "coincidence" because it is by such words that outwardly Bendrix explains such natural happenings; but in his writing, as opposed to his conversation, his defences go down.

There one sees the real conflict and how easily and often a man thinking he is feeling or acting from one set of motives is in actual fact feeling and acting from quite another set of motives. For each creature is a person at war with themselves—and none more so than either Bendrix or Sarah. As, alternatively, they pursue each other, so each of them is pursued inwardly: down the arches of the years and down the labyrinthine ways of their own minds. At one remove Greene has once more suggested how pursuit can become a means to salvation.

At the age of two it transpires that Sarah was baptized a Catholic—though she never knew of this herself. However, her mother when she had had her baptized hoped that in some manner it might "take" like an injection, and in her journal Sarah confesses that she has caught faith "like a disease." This somewhat clinical imagery is the counterpart of the idea of faith acting like "a twitch upon the thread" as it does in some of the novels of Maurice Baring and Evelyn Waugh. Yet Greene's more clinical imagery is probably better suited to a time which puts such trust in medicine as the curer of all physical and mental evils because it draws attention to the need for spiritual cures; at present when medicine makes bigger steps every day towards the abolishment of disease, it puts a check upon the belief now current that the only ills are physical and mental ones.

The End of the Affair brings home most forcibly this point in the way that it shows neither physical nor mental palliatives are enough to restore full harmony, to unite the double man. Physical and mental palliatives do not balance out, but must be drawn up and sublimated by the spirit so that they may become, as it were, the bases of a triangle. This is baldly stated, and Greene is far too much of an artist to make such dogmatic assertions in his fiction: rather, they appear as the natural corollaries from reading his books, especially his later ones. For in *The End of the Affair* Bendrix and Sarah in their pursuit are driven to look into themselves and to recognize—if only for a flash—in Whose Image they have been made. Which is why here, as in the rest of the Greene canon, pursuit for his characters so often becomes their means to salvation.

I have said that Greene is too much of an artist to make dogmatic theological assertions and though this is true of all his books, with the possible exception of *Brighton Rock* (1938),[9] one notices that the shadow of Newman's works lies heavily over those of Greene. Their point of departure is the same, and the three epigraphs which precede his travel book, *The Lawless Roads* (1939), include one from Cardinal Newman—the other two being picked from *Wit's Recreations* (1640) and Edwin Muir's poems. The passage from the *Apologia Pro Vita Sua* (1865) is worth quoting in full because it crystallizes Greene's attitude to men in a fallen world—an attitude of which in his reminiscences of his "lost childhood" one catches hints.

To consider the world in its length and breadth, its various history, the many races of man, their starts, their fortunes, their mutual alienation, their conflicts; and then their ways, habits, governments, forms of worship; their enterprises, their aimless courses, their random achievements and requirements, the impotent conclusion of long-standing facts, the tokens so faint and broken, of a superintending design, the blind evolution of what turn out to be great powers of truth, the progress of things, as if from unreasoning elements, not towards final causes, the greatness and littleness of man, his far-reaching aims, his short duration, the curtain hung over his futurity, the disappointments of life, the defeat of good, the success of evil, physical pain, mental anguish, the prevalence and intensity of sin, the pervading idolatries, the corruptions, the dreary hopeless irreligion, that condition of the whole race, so fearfully yet exactly described in the Apostle's words, "having no hope, and without God in the world"—all this is a vision to dizzy and appal; and inflicts upon the mind the sense of a profound mystery, which is absolutely beyond human solution.

What shall be said to this heart-piercing, reason-bewildering fact? I can only answer, that either there is no Creator, or this living society of men is in a true sense discarded from His presence. . . . *If* there be a God, *since* there is a God, the human race is implicated in some terrible aboriginal calamity.

Yet before Greene had even read Newman, he had as a boy read—"perhaps I was fourteen at the time"—Marjorie Bowen's *Viper of Milan* (1917), and that had crystallized once and for all his vision of men in a fallen world. "At the end of *The Viper of Milan,*" he recalled in a broadcast talk in 1947,[10] the great scene of "complete success" when

della Scala is dead, Ferrara, Verona, Novara, Mantua have all fallen. . . . Visconti sits and jokes in the wine light. I was not on the classical side or I would have discovered, I suppose, in Greek literature instead of in Miss Bowens novel, the sense of doom that lies over success—the feeling that the pendulum is about to swing. That too made sense; one looked around and saw the doomed everywhere—the champion runner who would one day sag over the tape; the head of the school who would atone, poor devil, during forty dreary undistinguished years.... Anyway she had given me my pattern—religion might later explain it to me in other terms, but the pattern was already there—perfect evil walking the world where perfect good can never walk again, and only the pendulum ensures that after all in the end justice will be done.

Newman's tokens, "so faint and broken, of a superintending design" were easy for Greene to accept because "the pattern was already there." His entry into the Catholic Church in 1926 was simply a religious confirmation of the fact. So it is that time and again in his dialogue one has the impression that it is as if he had translated Newman's ideas and thoughts into the language which his own characters would use were such thoughts and ideas to occur to them. There is no loss of spontaneity in the effect nor note of religious propaganda because in their contexts both ideas and thoughts appear logical enough. Indeed it is as if the dialogue were infused with a natural theology of its own, [11] so that throughout Greeneland—be it the tropical or asphalt jungle or, as it is now, "respectable" suburbia going seedy—his picture of men in a fallen world is not a pessimistic one, even though Hell may lie about their infancies. For continually is the hint projected through his characters that despair is not the final ending—even in Bendrix's prayer which served so well his wintry mood after Sarah's death: "O God, You've done enough. You've robbed me of enough, I'm too tired and old to learn to love, leave me alone for ever." Yet as Greene's chaplain says in *It's a Battlefield* (1934), despair can never be the final ending because "one can't hand in a resignation to God."

NOTES

1 W. H. Auden, *The Age of Anxiety* (New York: Random House, 1948).
2 Heinemann.

3 There is however one bad failure in characterization—Sarah's mother, Mrs. Bertram, who appears towards the close of the book. Of this failure Bendrix is himself quite aware, arguing that for the novelist there is always one character who is stillborn. This is a generalization which applies to all fiction and, indirectly writing at one remove, Greene has made a valuable point that (in an age which believes so much in the self-sufficiency of men unto themselves) deserves the widest hearing. Novelists are fallible and their work, no matter how visionary, because of original sin inevitably to some extent must be imperfect.

4 The effect of Bloy on Greene is apparent elsewhere. The last sentence of Bloy's novel, *La Femme Pauvre* (1897), reads: "She knew at the end there was only one unhappiness, and that is—NOT TO BE ONE OF THE SAINTS. In *The Power and the Glory* (1940), just before his execution, the whisky-priest also knows that 'at the end there was only one thing that counted—to be a saint.' "

5 There are other echoes from St. Augustine in Sarah's journal but this is the most pronounced one. (Cf. next footnote.)

6 Michael de la Bédoyère referring to the phrase "I'm a bitch and a fake and I hate myself" has suggested that this represents a new and more lively way of saying "I am a miserable sinner." In a sense and within its context Sarah's condemnation of herself once again echoes, though rather more faintly this time, some of St. Augustine's own self-condemnatory cries in the *Confessions.*

7 One recalls the Dryden epigraph from *The Power and the Glory*:

> Th' inclosure narrow'd; the sagacious power.
> Of hounds and death drew nearer every hour.

8 " 'I'm not sure. I've read somewhere these marks are hysterical in orgin. A mixture of psychiatry and radium.' It sounded plausible . . ." But at rock-bottom there is more doubt than certainty in Bendrix's mind about the plausibility of his reasoning.

9 In *Brighton Rock* there is a tendency for Greene to let the characters become archetypes of good and evil, right and wrong. If Pinkie and his girl Rose stand for good and evil, Ida, the cockney down from London, and her friend the detective stand for right and wrong: one feels that they are untroubled by sin, being interested simply in the "straight deal" and justice. They stand for law and order—that law

and order of which the police are the custodians. In contrast, Pinkie and Rose see their actions leading to either Heaven or Hell, salvation or damnation: they know that, even if they escape the police, they cannot escape God. This division appears inevitable in the construction of the plot, but its inevitability leads to a certain falsification in the novel as a work of art: it makes for a form of Catholic discrimination amongst the various characters which is nowhere apparent in any other of his novels or 'entertainments'.

10 The talk was entitled "Heroes are Made in Childhood" and was reprinted in *The Listener,* 27 March, 1947: it has subsequently been incorporated in Greene's book *The Lost Childhood and Other Essays* (1951).

11 Henry James drew upon psychological introspection for much of his best character-drawing and with L. H. Myers and E. M. Forster came into being what Maud Bodkin has christened the "philosophic novel." With Greene it has been whispered—notably on the Continent—that the advent of the 'theological novel' has come. I am distrustful. The grouping of fiction into such compartments tends to destroy a wholeness of vision in which "the real world of /Theology and horses" may be seen as different parts of one and the same universe. Greene is first and foremost a novelist with a number of stories to tell, and in those stories it is true that a number of theological points arise; but they arise in an untheological way. The implications are left to others to unravel—in the way for example that political speeches on atomic warfare also sometimes raise problems for the theologians to unravel. In *The End of the Affair* Smythe, the West London rationalist preacher is disturbed by the power of Christianity. He feels that every denial of it is only a stronger affirmation of its power to survive in the Western World so that one cannot even say "good-bye" to anyone without, consciously or unconsciously, saying "God be with you." Now this is a novelist's observation, lending itself to the thought that since "between the stirrup and the ground there's often mercy found" many rationalists and unbelievers may discover, having unwittingly invoked God's protection of their friends, that at the last in His infinite mercy He will be with them. Yet Greene does not develop the thought thus far, but merely hints at it. What theological implications there are in it is left for others to unravel: his function as Smythe's creator is simply to think as Smythe would—nothing more.

R. E. Hughes

THE QUIET AMERICAN: THE CASE REOPENED

Perhaps now the furor over Graham Greene's novel, *The Quiet American,* has died down to the point that analysis on a non-political basis can proceed. When the novel first appeared [several] years ago, too many readers were quick to discover, or to invent, evidence that here was a bit of anti-American propaganda, a piece of British smugness triumphing over American naiveté; and the air grew so thick with jingoism that the novel *qua* novel was considerably obscured.

The point most obscured, unfortunately, was the complexity of Greene's narrative technique. *The Quiet American* reveals Greene's most advanced use of dramatic irony in the novel form, and once the reader recognizes that Fowler is not Greene's *alter ego,* but a character being observed and criticized by both reader and author, then the novel as chauvinism disappears, and the novel as art emerges. For Fowler is no spokesman for the British conscience or for Greene the Union Jack-waver; he is a figure being patiently dissected by the novelist and diagnosed as pitifully sterile in a sterile situation, confronted time and again with the cure for his sickness but unable to comprehend it. Briefly, Fowler is a prime example of the obtuse narrator: the story-teller who offers his experiences without fully understanding them, while at the same time providing the less obtuse reader with the complete evidence.

A perfunctory reading of the novel suggests that Greene is working on a variation of so many of Henry James'

Reprinted by permission of *Renascence,* XII (Autumn, 1959).

novels: the innocent American confronted by the wise but decadent European. A closer examination reveals that there is no confronting. As a matter of fact, there is no real *rapport* anywhere in the novel. "How I wished there existed someone to whom I could say that I was sorry" is the last remark of the book, and here lies the real theme. Fowler is a total alien: an Englishman in Indo-China with no home to return to. Pyle, the quiet American, is chronically alien, not only to Indo-China, but to the whole pragmatic, un-ideal world in which he must live. Phuong, Fowler's mistress, "was wonderfully ignorant: if Hitler had come into the conversation she would have interrupted to ask who he was,"—a clear example of the provincial alienated from the rest of the world. Again and again there are allusions to and emblems of apartness and isolation: Fowler's escape from the world through opium; the language barrier which exists between Pyle and the natives; the press conference where the correspondents are addressed through an interpreter in terms which do not square with what they have experienced; the mud tower, alone on an empty field, in which Pyle and Fowler crouch under attack; Pyle's lonely death.

This is the nerve which Greene's novel touches: the problem which Sartre perceives with desperation, which Camus explores with discomfort, and which psychologists and sociologists have defined as perhaps the most serious malady of our culture. Where does individual existence leave off and social responsibility begin? Greene's novel asks the question, and then transcends it. *The Quiet American* is an account of various attempts to solve the problem; and Greene's irony is most operative in this, that none of the solutions explicitly proposed is satisfactory, and none of the major characters recognizes the true solution which the reader is led to discover.

How does one bridge the gap between selfish existence and social unity? Pyle's solution is economic humanitarianism; but good will and dollars are inadequate, even disastrous. But if such an abstract formula is a failure, so too are merely human measures. As he did in *The Heart of the Matter* and *The Power and the Glory,* Greene shows how human pity can bridge the gap between individuals. For all his insistence that he wants to remain disengaged, detached from the world, Fowler is made to feel in union with mankind through his sense of pity: pity for the family needlessly wiped out in a raid; pity for the mother modestly covering the body of her mutilated child; pity for the death of Pyle; pity even for the raucous Granger, prostrated by news of his son's illness. But all these *rapprochements* are momentary; they all fail to provide Fowler with a remedy for his sense of ennui and loneliness.

Obtuse as he is, Fowler does not recognize the one spokesman for an adequate participation in humanity: the priest in the blood-speckled soutane. The scene is so brief, so undeveloped, that the casual reader might ask if it is relevant. The reply would be: what are the priest's motives for his becoming so absorbed with humanity, as protector, confessor, and surgeon?

The import of such details is focused, I believe, in a symbol so traditional and so conservative as to be surprising, even daring, in a contemporary novel; a symbol as antique as the mediaeval bestiaries, those collections of allegorical fables designed to elucidate religious doctrine. The symbol is that of the Phoenix as the resurrected Christ. And to carry the implications of the symbol further, Christ resurrected is the Catholic symbol of corporate unity, dramatic proof of the Mystical Body. "We are all one in Christ" is the unspoken working belief of the priest in the bloody soutane. The central figure in the novel is Fowler, the seeker of birds; and his mistress' name Phuong, "means Phoenix, but nothing nowadays is fabulous, and nothing rises from its ashes." With characteristic short-sightedness, Fowler fails to recognize the symbol. In a manner of speaking, he is content to grasp the girl and overlooks that there has been a fabulous rising which would dispel his apartness from humanity.

The final irony of the novel lies in the fact that Fowler

does not have the vision to carry out what may be called the Augustinian pattern of conversion, the flight from and through sensual corporateness into a sense of divine union with all men (a pattern Greene had already used in *The End of the Affair.*) The sadness of *The Quiet American* is not that Pyle should die, but that Fowler should have been blind to the only adequate solution of his problem, insoluble by Pyle's economics, by Vigot's quietism, by his own human pity.

This novel of Greene's is, to repeat what was said at the beginning, his most advanced use to date of dramatic irony as a technique. Failing to see the irony, we fail to see the real theme of the novel, and consequently fail to see a most impressive argument for the Catholicism of Greene's art.

Alice Mayhew

THE COMEDIANS

There are two tragic characters in Graham Greene's *The Comedians*: Magiot, an elderly Negro communist who believes in life and the future and is shot down in the end by the state police; and poor "Haiti itself and the character of Doctor Duvalier's rule . . . not even blackened for dramatic effect." All the others are the comedians of the title—plastic as masks, non-committal as movie stars, clumsy and sad as clowns. These are the strolling players, extras and spectators to the real world, the cop-outs and the watery-thin dreamers. This is, at least, how they seem most of the time, and most particularly to Brown who is protagonist, narrator, non-hero and the latest Greene character to be on the wrong end of a game of dodge 'em with God.

The Comedians is, in many ways, more complicated than Greene's previous novels, and the least Jansenistic and most optimistic. There remain the central preoccupations of his morality plays, but in this latest novel Greene achieves qualities of humility, humor and intellectuality that are mellower than ever before. He seems to have been moving toward this book since *The End of the Affair,* and certainly noticeably through *The Burnt-Out Case.* The protagonists of these two books were less sentimentally drawn and more rationalist than either Scobie (*The Heart of the Matter*) or the whiskey priest from *The Power and the Glory.*

Bendrix in the first, energetically hated that God whom he rightly recognized as the source of his defeat. Querry,

Reprinted from *The National Catholic Reporter,* March 30, 1966.

in *The Burnt-Out Case,* with one foot in the sacristy and the other in the salon, has a pervading sense of his serio-comic position as a man, of the world's absurdity, of the possibility that farce can break out even in the *sanctum sanctorum* and reduce religion to slapstick. He is, in short, something of a special kind of modern existentialist. Not entirely, however. The atheist Doctor Colin accuses him, correctly, of fingering his lack of faith like a sore. This is a quality of the familiar Greene advocate. Querry however is rather abstract, a case-study, a query. *The Burnt-Out Case* lacked the tension and implacability of *The End of the Affair;* Querry had less fiber than Bendrix.

In his preface to *The Burnt-Out Case,* Greene wrote that it was "an attempt to give dramatic expression to various types of belief, half-belief, and non-belief in the kind of setting removed from world politics and household preoccupation, where such differences are felt acutely and find expression." *The Comedians* is more *engage* with the real world and it takes place not in a state of mind but, as Greene wrote, in "poor Haiti itself." In this book Greene moves out of the Catholic ghetto—it would seem for good—and shows a fresh gentleness and patience with the sad lot who populate it.

There is self-mockery, as well as self-parody in this novel. The setting provides a general, exteriorized hell—like the hell of Scobie built for himself in his own mind. In *The End of the Affair* Bendrix loses Sarah to God, the superior Plotmaker; and his successor Querry loses his life in a vignette of bedroom farce. The latest novel takes up all these strains and intensifies and mocks them at the same time.

One might say, for example, that Brown—a middle-aged transient, a failure and a rootless man who comes to Haiti when he is summoned by a telegram from a mother he has not seen for over two decades, and stays when he inherits her hotel—inhabits a world that is made-to-order for a Greene protagonist, for it is hell-on-earth. It is the place that Greene described in his essay, "The Lost Childhood," in which "perfect evil (walks) the world where perfect good can never walk again, and only the pendulum ensures that after all in the end justice is done." Greene, however, now re-conceives this world as comic as well as tragic. "A reign of terror," he wrote when describing Haiti in an English newspaper, "has often about it the atmosphere of farce. The irresponsible is in control. The banana skin is a deadly one, but it remains a banana skin. From the moment you land from an airplane in Port-au-Prince—that city of ruined elegance where the houses belong to the world of Charles Addams and the door may well be opened to you by a Boris Karloff. . . ."

In *The Comedians,* even the pervasive cruelty and ill-health of the corrupt regime is dualized in the legend that Dr. Duvalier is really Baron Samedi. As Baron Samedi, a Voodoo spirit, this personage dressed in top hat and tails haunts the cemeteries at night; during the day, as Dr. Duvalier, he hides in the presidential palace from his enemies. The Doctor has a force of smaller bad spirits, headed by the dark archangel, Captain Concasseur ("Steamroller"), who is straight from the boards of a black comedy. They have all enjoyed a long run.

This theme of farce and theatricality seizes the whole book. Brown talks incessantly of *melodrama, personages, plot complications* when he means *life, friends* and *events.* This element of farce works perfectly for the burden of this story which, more rationalist than Greene's past themes, turns on the question of identity—an identity which is not imposed from the outside by fiat, or even by God and His sacraments, but grown on the rocky soil of essential ambiguity and paradox. The central inquiry here is identity as vocation, as act.

Moreover, this novel is the most socially conscious of Greene's works; these people do not live in a state of theological evaluation but in the real political world. Here, the enemy of goodness is indifference, and though a Manichean evil still roams the world, it is a little frivolous and the most vivid struggles are between right and wrong, rather than good and evil. Brown would not be apt to describe the void of loneliness and disillusion in which he lives as a dark night of the soul. It is plain that Brown is in no way exceptional to modern man. He is, indeed, almost fatally nondescript, and his world, Haiti, "(is) not an exception in a sane world: it was a small slice of everyday taken at random."

There is also a trinity of specific parodies. The narrator Brown creates roles for everyone, plays one and even several himself, and believes in nothing else. He is half late-Greene, and half early-Greene—urbane, indifferent, sardonic, and yet he is also the old priest *manque,* dispossessed believer, God's victim and quarry. Secondly, there is Smith, the vegetarian, ex-Freedom Rider and minor candidate for the presidency in Truman's year. Smith desires to be man's savior by releasing him from his passions with a vegetable and fruit diet, and he has come to Haiti with his wife to establish a vegetarian center. ("Eliminate acidity and you give a kind of elbow room to the conscience.") The third member of this trinity is Jones, a rather off-beat symbol of love, since he, most unlikely, inspires it everywhere, much to Brown's disgust. Jones appears in the world under various guises, a simple matter since he is a cheat and racketeer; in this episode he is a fake British major.

The elderly Smith, whose middle name is Abel, also takes on two other roles; his is, here, *the* American type, and as well the familiar Greene Innocent. Frank Kermode has pointed out that innocence and pity are great enemies of human happiness in Greene. It is probably because they represent options for fantasy rather than realism, sentimentality rather than harsh judgments, self-indulgence in place of selflessness. Still, Greene is tolerant of the Smiths, and allows us to see the valiance behind their bland naivete. They somewhat resemble Fowler, from *The Quiet American,* committing charities designed more to comfort themselves than to aid the recipients, and forgetful of the realities of the brute world. And yet they can be courageous and cheeky when they are up against an evil they espy, and they even spy it with a certain shrewdness.

Brown, having lost his identity (he was educated, and then thrown out by the Jesuits and has ended up faithless) has given up hope of finding another, and contents himself with little roles and schemes. Smith's vocation—as well as his identification as "the presidential candidate"—is, whatever his personal merit, frankly foolish. Jones, on the other hand, is the admitted comedian. He willingly plays his roles, takes a publicly wry attitude about himself and finally, dies a tragi-comic death when he finds a role to play that he can freely admire. This occurs when he takes on the job of leading some incompetent guerillas against Duvalier. He falls behind because of his flat feet, and is killed. Brown has tricked him into the position because of a supposed affair between Jones and Brown's mistress. (The familiar Greene syndrome of the lover's curious, ill-founded and self-consuming jealousy is repeated in this novel.) Still, Jones, who knows very well that he is being thrust into a role he cannot possibly hope to fit, thanks Brown for giving him his "big chance." The circuit stops when a man can settle down to something, anything, he can care about. The only hero from start to finish is the elderly Doctor Magiot who is a committed Marxist—a man of definite hopes and decided personal aspirations.

One of the most startling of Greene's parodies in this novel is the character of Brown's mistress Martha, the wife of a Latin-American diplomat and the daughter of a Nazi war criminal. She is a dead-ringer for Sarah (*The End of the Affair*) by temperament, mannerism, fluke and husband-type, except that she performs her function (of moving the drama along) in a less dramatic fashion than Sarah. She is a shadowy character, present only in the rather banal love scenes, and as a device. (There are no important woman characters in Greene; they are all means to ends. Even Sarah is incidental to *The End of the Affair* since the epic battle is between Bendrix and

God.) Martha puts Jones on the path to his vocation and serves Brown's as well by being a piece of evidence that the world is not only independent but frequently at odds with his conception of it. Brown, in fact, levels the lethal Greene charge at her: she has not lost her innocence; she is uninvolved. If Brown undergoes a change—and we sense rather than know it—it is that he loses his innocence. He is brought into an embrace with the real world, commits himself to it, prepares to act in it in some way, freely.

There is another trinity of clear moral intent. The first is a Voodoo ceremony, the second is a Catholic priest's sermon and the third an epistle from the communist doctor, Magiot. All of these urge involvement even at the cost of violence, a reason for faith, and a context for action. The Voodoo ceremony, filled with prayers from the Latin Mass—*libera nos a malo,* with the gods of Dahomey; *agnus dei,* with a sacrifice of a censer-trussed cock; *corruptio optimi,* with the transformation of a lame servant into the personification of an avenging warrior—encourages a revolt against the dictator.

The young priest at Mass also preaches a message of action and commitment: "Let us go up to Jerusalem and die with Him. The Church is in the world, it is part of the suffering of the world, and though Christ condemned the servant who struck off the ear of the high priest's servant, our hearts go out in sympathy to all who are moved to violence by the suffering of others. Violence can be the expression of love, indifference never. One is an imperfection of charity, the other the perfection of egoism."

The third message is the posthumous letter from Magiot to Brown after the communist, who is not a conspirator, has been killed by the Tentons Macoute, the state bogeymen, as a gesture of friendship to the American CIA. He tells Brown that there is always an alternative to the faith one has lost, and that one must choose action: "Catholics and communists have committed great crimes, but at least they have not stood aside, like an established society, and been indifferent. I would rather have blood on my hands than water like Pilate. . . ." This message takes us back more to the drunkard priest of *The Power and the Glory,* than to the victimized prisoners of God's dispositions that populate other Greene novels. But there is an extremely typical Greene disposition here as well. Like Sarah, who was baptized without her knowledge and who therefore had already on her soul the mark of the Church and of salvation, Brown too is *predisposed* to faith—if not to one, then to another (the same faith under different masks) and Magiot makes no bones on this point. He reminds Brown that, "We are humanists, you and I." As Sarah is the unwitting daughter of the God she doesn't know, so Brown is the son of a mother he did not know, but who was loved by Magiot, and who is depicted as an intensely concerned and possibly heroic person. "You won't admit it," he writes, "but you are the son of your mother and you once took that dangerous journey *which we all have to take before the end.*" (Italics mine)

Greene's references and emphasis have changed somewhat but not on one central fact. There is still no escape from the vocation to will, act, love, to be sanctified. After the Voodoo ceremony, Brown remarks that he had not shed his Catholic God just to become a *victim* of the gods of Dahomey. (That is the mark of the Greene protagonist; he may be God's antagonist, but he is also his lawful victim.) Nevertheless, something's got Brown, even if it is only the common sense of Magiot, or his admiration for the only committed man in the cast of characters. If you don't volunteer for the army of the *engages* on either side, you are drafted—there are deferments, but no permanent excuses.

There is much in Greene, even some of the characters, that has scarcely changed. What has evolved is a way of looking at the world, which makes it possible to see more, a view which reveals the world as filled with farcical, impertinent, confusing strains. His tone has become more humanist, less dogmatic, more compassionate, less arrogant. "Now that I approached the end of life," Brown says, "it was only my sense of humor that enabled me to believe in Him. Life was a comedy, not the tragedy for which I had been prepared, and it seemed to me that we were all . . . driven by an authorative practical joker towards an extreme point of comedy."

Suggested Additional Readings

Consolo, Dominick. "Music as Motif: The Unity of *Brighton Rock*," *Renascence*, XV (Fall, 1962), pp. 12-20.

Evans, Robert. "Existentialism in Greene's *The Quiet American*," *Modern Fiction Studies*, III (Autumn, 1957), pp. 241-248.

Evans, Robert (ed.). *Graham Greene, Some Critical Considerations*. Lexington: University of Kentucky Press, 1963.

Glicksberg, Charles. "Graham Greene: Catholicism in Fiction," *Criticism*, I (Fall, 1959), pp. 339-353.

Kunkel, Francis. *The Labyrinthine Ways of Graham Greene*. New York: Sheed and Ward, 1959.

Markovic, Vida. "Graham Greene in Search of God," *Texas Studies in Literature and Language*," V (Summer, 1963), pp. 271-282.

CONTRIBUTORS

NEVILLE BRAYBROOKE, the British scholar, is the author of *T. E. Eliot*. His writings have appeared in *Commonweal, The English Journal* and many other periodicals.

HARRY J. CARGAS is the General Editor of the Christian Critic Series and is the Director of Orientation, U.S.A., St. Louis University. He has published articles and reviews in over fifty periodicals.

DOMINICK P. CONSOLO is Chairman of Honors Seminars at Denison University. He obtained his doctorate from the State University of Iowa and was a Reader for the National Council of Teachers of English.

R. E. HUGHES has published *John Joyne's Journal* and *Rhetoric: Principles and Usage*. His doctorate is from the University of Wisconsin. He is Chairman of the English Department, Boston College.

MARY EVELYN JEFFERSON was a student at the University of North Carolina when she wrote the essay contained in this volume. She now teaches at Stratford College, Danville, Va.

R. W. B. LEWIS is perhaps best known for *The American Adam* and *The Picaresque Saint*. He is also the editor of *Herman Melville* (*A Reader*).

ALICE MAYHEW is a graduate of Fordham University and did graduate work at the Sorbonne. She is an editor at Random House whose writings have appeared in *Commonweal* and *National Catholic Reporter*.

KARL PATTEN, who earned his Ph.D. at Boston University, is currently located at Bucknell.

ROGER POOLE did his doctoral thesis on Kierkegaard at Cambridge. For two years he lectured at the Sorbonne, in Paris, and is currently at the University of Nottingham.

CAROLYN SCOTT is the co-editor of the book on Gerard Manley Hopkins in this series. She has been on the faculty at the University of Kentucky, Washington University and Fontbonne College.